# AT
# MY FATHER'S
# WEDDING

# AT MY FATHER'S WEDDING

## Reclaiming Our True Masculinity

## John Lee

**BANTAM BOOKS**

NEW YORK • TORONTO • LONDON • SYDNEY • AUCKLAND

AT MY FATHER'S WEDDING

*A Bantam Book/November 1991*

*Grateful acknowledgment is made for permission to reprint the*
*following: Excerpt from "On My Father's Wedding, 1924," from*
The Man in the Black Coat Turns *by Robert Bly. Copyright © 1981 by*
*Robert Bly. Used by permission of Doubleday, a division of Bantam*
*Doubleday Dell Publishing Group, Inc. Excerpt from "Do Not Go*
Gentle Into That Good Night" *from* Poems of Dylan Thomas *by Dylan*
*Thomas. Copyright 1952 by Dylan Thomas. Reprinted by permission of*
*New Directions Publishing Corporation.*

*Book design and project supervision by*
*M'N O Production Services, Inc.*

**Library of Congress Cataloging-in-Publication Data**
Lee, John H., 1951–
    At my father's wedding : men healing themselves and each other/
John Lee.
        p.     cm.
    Includes bibliographical references.
    ISBN 0-553-07730-9
    1. Men—Psychology.   2. Fathers and sons.   3. Masculinity
(Psychology)   I. Title.
HQ1090.L44    1991
305.31—dc20                                         91–18478
                                                          CIP

*Published simultaneously in the United States and Canada*

*Bantam Books are published by Bantam Books, a division of Bantam*
*Doubleday Dell Publishing Group, Inc. Its trademark, consisting of the*
*words "Bantam Books" and the portrayal of a rooster, is Registered in U.S.*
*Patent and Trademark Office and in other countries. Marca Registrada.*
*Bantam Books, 666 Fifth Avenue, New York, New York 10103.*

*PRINTED IN THE UNITED STATES OF AMERICA*
BVG      0 9 8 7 6 5 4 3 2 1

DEDICATED TO:

My Partners—My Friends Forever

Dan Jones, Bill Stott, Marvin Allen,

Allen Maurer, and John Hunger

ALSO TO:

The men who have taught, healed, or loved me so much:

Caleb Curren, Deryle Perryman, Roger Fuller, Bob White,

Dane Dixon, Rick Rose, Lyman Grant, Robert Bly,

Wayne Kritsberg, and Melvin Kenne.

The title of this book was inspired by a reading of Robert Bly's poem, "On My Father's Wedding 1924." While this is not a book about Robert Bly or his work, it would not have been written were it not for many of his words.

# CONTENTS

## PART TWO: THE JOURNEY

## PART FOUR: THE FUTURE

# ACKNOWLEDGMENTS

Without the support and love of these people this book would not have been written: My two editors—Linda Loewenthal, who brought me to Bantam and helped me make a fragmented dream into concrete chapters, and Leslie Meredith, who gently guided those chapters into more chapters and finally a reality. I'm forever grateful to them both.

Also, I am deeply grateful to two partners and friends: Bill Stott for his continued support of my work, and Beverly Barnes, who loved to listen, listened with love, and supported me and my writing.

Much thanks to my assistant Jodi Roberts, who made my life easier and worked almost as hard as I did to make this book appear.

A special and warm thanks to the men who shared their stories and souls with me.

My deepest appreciation goes to Marvin Allen for his partnership in his Wildman Gatherings and Dan Jones, my partner in men's groups for six years.

My heartfelt thanks to my Higher Power—God/Goddess—for allowing me the opportunity to share, smile, cry, be angry, forgive, and move toward deeper healing with all who read this and all who don't.

# PREFACE

M any thousands of men are finally willing to stop denying that we are in pain. We have begun to listen to the hurts that run through our bodies like the blood through our veins. More and more of us are ready to go deep into our souls to find a father-wound that we have always known was there but have been afraid to feel. We are ready to seek the missing father who lies deeply buried in each of us, the dad we lost to work, routine, drugs, alcohol, wars, TV, and the mind-numbing pursuit of money and all the things that could be bought with it.

We are ready to feel the truth that our fathers were not there for us emotionally, physically, or spiritually—or at all. Because they were not there for us as children or as adults, we feel our fathers' absence more than their presence; and because as sons we are reflections—in positive or negative ways—of our fathers, their absence creates a feeling of absence within us, a feeling that we do not know or understand ourselves, a feeling of loss, woundedness, deadness, and abandonment.

A German psychologist, Alexander Mitscherlich, said once, Where the father is absent from the son's life, a hole forms and demons rush in to fill that hole. Men are ready to acknowledge that hole in our lives, to descend into that dark chasm and begin the lengthy process of exorcising the demons we allowed in when our fathers failed us. We are finished stuffing that void with the same demons, obsessions, or dependencies with which our fathers filled their own emptiness to avoid feeling it. We are ready to begin healing ourselves and reclaiming our true masculinity.

*At My Father's Wedding* looks at men as they take this journey inward to find and heal themselves. It shows men at different starting points, men with many different stories, but men who all share the determination to understand and improve their lives and relationships. I hope this book will also provide insight and guidance to men who want to take this crucial initiatory trek but who are unsure—or completely in the dark—about how to begin. I want to encourage and entice reluctant, but otherwise ready men to go deeper inside themselves and find the wounds they've kept buried for so long, to discover the peace, freedom, and healing that comes with the attainment of their individual definitions of true manhood.

This book is about the wonderful magic that comes when one is finally able to feel good about being a man. And it is about the joy that comes with the discovery and acceptance of one's "deep masculinity," as well as an acknowledgment of one's feminine side.

While it is a book for and about men, *At My Father's*

Wedding may also assist women in finding bits and pieces of themselves to help make them whole. At their deepest levels, these pages are about the masculinity and femininity found in both men and women. Since I have never had a woman's body or mind, however, I'll be speaking as a man and will not apologize for the bias inherent in the voice and vision I record. I will also speak from my experience which, regarding sexual preference, is a heterosexual one. I hope, however, that gay men will be able to relate to what "straight" men have to say.

One of the many reasons I wrote this book was to make concrete somehow what I've learned, felt, heard, shared, and saved thus far from the hundreds of hours well spent in the company of men in men's gatherings and workshops, in my private moments with my men friends and colleagues, in my very trying and expensive inner journey toward my own masculinity, and in my recovery from my own troubled childhood as I worked through the trauma of living with an absent and abusive father.

Another reason I wrote it was to share what goes on in men's workshops, when men leave women, jobs, and families for a while to join a group of other men who are committed to growing beyond stereotypes, to healing old wounds, and to recovering their lost souls and increasing and deepening their sense of self. I wrote it to help further the growing men's movement and to help men find a safe passage through largely unexplored terrain, and for all those women who have told me how much they'd give to "be a fly on the wall" at men's gatherings. Although women don't belong in men's groups, just as men do not belong in women's groups, it is crucial that women understand, value, and support the difficult work men are only just beginning to do.

When men who are leading men's groups, retreats, gatherings, and conferences are asked if they are part of the "men's movement," some reply, "What men's movement?" or, "What is a men's movement?" or even, simply, "No." And each of their answers is correct, for the "men's movement" is not a movement organized around some particular socio-economic or political ideology. While men's centers are being formed, conferences and gatherings are being scheduled all around the United States and in Western Europe, and books, magazines, and journals addressing men's issues are appearing weekly, the men's movement as I see it is a philosophical, spiritual, and emotional movement. Its philosophy is so broad that it allows many men and women from different backgrounds and with different issues to remove individual cancerous behaviors, patterns, and injustices. It's an emotional movement, a releasing of the pain and poison men have been holding in their collective stomachs for centuries. It is not power-oriented in any way, but powerful in that it frees men and their spirits from the tyranny of the old paradigm of "Don't feel. Die younger than women. Don't talk. Don't grieve. Don't get angry. Don't rock the boat. Don't trust other men. Don't put passion before bill paying. Follow the crowd, not your bliss." The movement is creating a new paradigm as I write, and it is helping men to take responsibility for their pain instead of projecting it onto others, to learn how to be friends with men, to love their children and partners, and to grieve the loss of childhood and their fathers. Men are being moved to act on behalf of their planet and to reclaim the energy that soul-snatching bureaucracies, factories, and technologies have been gleaning from them for decades as fuel to keep the wheels of industry and government going.

Yes, there is a men's movement and you are part of it. You, I, and men and women all over the country are breaking down the notion that to be a man is a bad thing. When the tears pour out and men let go of years of anger and hurt, that's powerful. It's powerful to watch. It's powerful to be a part of.

*At My Father's Wedding* is a short book about a lifelong journey. It is a collection of thoughts, feelings, and experiences in short pieces with interwoven themes; its organization is organic. It arises truthfully out of my own experiences as well as those of men I have known and counseled. It may seem a prose poem at its best and assembled fragments at its worst, just as a man's own life, if lived well, should resemble a poem full of sound and fury and finally signifying something more than how much he earned and how many toys he bought at the expense of time spent with people he loved. At its worst, during the self-discovery and healing process, a man's life will at times be chaotic and confused, although he will no longer feel crazy, addicted, or dead. And, as he gains an identity and recovers his deep masculinity, his life will take on a semblance of beauty and coherence.

I hope this book enlivens all who read it and offers a little light to those who have begun or are about to begin walking the healing path. I thank the men who have enlivened me by entrusting me with their truth, stories, pain, and passion, which are all so much a part of this book. I have been very careful not to reveal their identities and have kept their privacy and trust intact by changing names, descriptions, and locations while staying true to the book's purpose. And I thank all you readers for choosing to join me and these men who are your brothers, lovers, husbands, sons, and friends for the next several hours.

Here is some of what you can expect to find in *At My Father's Wedding*: A deeper understanding of why men are so far away from themselves and their feelings, their fathers, each other, and the women they love; why many men need to go into men's groups or into the woods with other men, take off their armor, and peel off their layers of pain and sadness in the company of men. I'll also try to explain: Why men long for relationships with women that are equal and healthy and yet fear them so much, why many men who chase women are like dogs who chase cars—they catch them and then don't know what to do with them; why during workshop meditations, men and women cry and scream silently or out loud when I simply say the words "father," "dad," or "daddy." And, we will explore why men are turning out in unprecedented numbers at men's workshops, supporting men's centers, and filling men's groups; why now, of all times, they are ready to work on themselves and take an equal measure of responsibility for mending their wounds and their relationships; and why men need to heal, feel, and be with each other, holding out supporting hands and arms to one another. Finally, we'll try to understand why some men are still afraid to come out of their denial of their pain and alienation and so continue to foist their woundedness and dysfunction on women, family, society, and the earth.

When we go into unfamiliar terrain—whether physical or psychological, whether a forest or a men's group, we not only need maps, we need guides as well. In this book, we will work with some of the ideas of two of my favorite guides, C. G. Jung and Robert Bly, as well as with new and traditional psychological ideas, including ideas from Eastern spirituality, mythology, poetry, and Twelve-Step recovery philosophy. All of these sources will help us get in touch with our anger and our grief. I will also place a heavy emphasis on the body, as well as the emotions, for, in my opinion, men's bodies have been overlooked and numbed in many of the healing journeys on which they embark. We have to learn again how to feel and be comfortable in our bodies, to overcome our well-learned tendencies to deny physical pain, fatigue, or exhaustion, for our bodies store the missing parts of our past, the parts we must remember in order to heal in the present.

So, as you read these pages, don't forget to breathe. Breathing brings us into our bodies and centers us in the moment. Take a deep breath before you read on, to clear your mind and prepare yourself for a dive into your deeper being. Take several deep breaths as you read through each page and I promise it will make the journey gentler and easier.

Now join me as we go to the bottom of the well of our grief, descend into the fire of our appropriate anger, and then ascend to our true potential and the joy that we and others have denied ourselves for so long.

# PART ONE

# THE WOUND

# THE LOST FATHER

## Our Deepest Wound

S ometimes a man wakes up in the middle of the night, or disappears emotionally in the middle of love-making, or stops repairing a motor because he misses his father. Sometimes the longing is so painful that he has a few drinks, smokes a cigarette, or goes and exercises the sadness away. He does anything he can to escape feeling the emptiness.

Other times, he finds a woman who reminds him of his father—unavailable, distant, and cold. He loves her like the father he grew up with. He wants to fix her and make her be there for him, to close the distance and warm him like his father forgot to do—or couldn't do. Of course, the woman can't fix him, and he can't change or control her any more than he could his father. But he tries just the same.

At other times, if he's tired of trying to close the distance with a dance-away lover, he resorts to finding a woman who lets him be the center of her universe. She clings to him and his every word, something his father never did, never thought about doing. Ironically, he will try to teach her how to be less available by adopting his dad's behaviors: he's late for supper or parties, forgetful of special occasions, and emotionally unavailable. When he acts like his father in these ways, he misses him less since now he *is* his dad. Unable to close the gap in any other way, he joins forces psychologically with his father, and feels less vulnerable, less alone.

In his longing, he also turns other men into his father. The other day at one of my men's gatherings a young man approached me. "We need to talk," he said somewhat abruptly. I thought, "Here it comes," for whenever someone (especially someone I don't know) tells me that "we" need to talk, I know "I" don't and "they" do. And the talk is usually not about "me" as much as it is about them and their history. "I've been here the whole weekend, and I've tried to make eye contact with you, and you keep avoiding me. Why won't you look at me? Why are you avoiding me?" he said as his voice and fear rose an octave.

I looked directly into his intense blue eyes and asked, "Would you be willing to try an experiment with me?" He hesitated for a moment and then said, "Yes."

"Okay, here it goes. I'm going to ask you a question and you give me the first thought or feeling that comes up." I took a deep breath. "Who are you?"

His blue eyes were immediately bathed in tears. "You don't know me, do you?" he asked.

4

"No, I don't, and I'm looking you right in the eyes as I say this. I don't know you, so I can't be avoiding you. I might avoid you once I know you, but I'm not doing it this weekend. Do you see what's happening?"

Another tear ran down his cheek. "I guess I got some father stuff to deal with. My dad never paid any attention to me. He could never look me in the eye."

Sometimes my own eyes long to see my father so much that I turn men who are simply living their own lives the best they can into fathers. Every so often I'll put in a call to Robert Bly and wait for weeks before I hear from him, if I hear from him at all. During that time I'll think, "Well to hell with him. If he ain't got time to return my calls, who needs him anyway." At that moment I turn Robert into Jimmy Lee, the man who never had enough time for me. And I stop being forty years old and hover around the age of thirteen.

Other men may give their allegiance to gurus, countries, political parties, and corporations, allegiances that they willingly would have given their fathers if they had not been so angry at them. The guru, sponsor, or "spiritual teacher" may tell men how many kids to have, where to work, when to marry, when to divorce. The country tells them when to go to war, when to die, when to kill, when to stop killing. The political party tells them when to campaign, when to rally, when to vote yes, when to vote no. And the corporation tells them where to live, who to entertain, when to abstain, and when to hire. The corporation also tells men when they're no longer productive and need to be terminated. So the corporation becomes a negative father substitute, a father who destroys instead of reinforcing his "sons," manipulating them for his own gain. Allegiance to a corporation usually deepens the father wound and sense of loss.

## WAITING FOR THE FATHER

Men find many substitutes for the fatherly teaching, advice, wisdom, and warnings they were never given because Dad was never there.

Some men miss their dead fathers so much that rather than burying them emotionally and going on with their lives, they keep them alive in their own heads. The father's voice lives and speaks where the son's sounds should be. The son knows the voice and turns up the volume, particularly in times of crisis and stress, or when he has simply screwed up. The voice says, "You're not working hard enough"; "When are you going to get a real job?"; or, "When I was your age . . ."

By letting the father sit on the throne of our psyches and souls, we keep ourselves from living. We see Dad and his judgments everywhere and thus don't see ourselves as we really are, or others as they really are. If our father is alive, many of us keep providing him with opportunities to be the dad he couldn't be in the fifties or the sixties and surely cannot be in the nineties. So many men want their dads to be there for them that they keep creating opportunities for these fathers to say how much they love their son or to ask them for advice. But the love and reaching out from father to son never come. What do come are the same old sounds, "I'll loan you this money to buy a house, but I want to come check out the different areas of town to make sure that you get the best deal for my money." Or, cruelly, they say, "The day I have to listen to advice from the likes of you will be a cold day in hell, young man."

Some men wait and purposely do not make enough money to buy the house they want in order to give dear old Dad one more chance to come through for them. Some sons wait until it's too late to walk up to Dad before he dies to say, "Dad, I want you to tell me that you love me." And some will wait and never offer Dad any advice at all, whether it's about when to plant cucumbers or how to set up an I.R.A., even if the son has an agricultural degree from Iowa State or a business degree from Harvard. Some sons wait eternally for their dads to become the dad they never had. They freeze themselves forever in a powerless, childlike role in which they never feel happy, satisfied, or personally competent. They wait for their fathers to die and when they do die, they wait as long as they possibly can before they let themselves feel the grief.

The substitute dads, the unsatisfying relationships, the voices in our heads, the waiting—all are forms of missing the father. All are ways that men keep on being their father's son, their father's little boy. By refusing to grieve the loss of the father we never had, by continuing to find women and men who act like Dad, by giving the father in our own brains full reign over our bodies, by allowing him to determine the work we do, how we earn a living, or when we go to war, by refusing to bury once and for all the ghost father who looms at night in our houses, businesses, and dreams, we do not allow ourselves our rightful manhood, our individual achievements, success, or identities. To break this powerless pattern of waiting and wanting, to move from this childlike, impotent state into manhood, re-

requires letting go of our childlike expectations. We must say good-bye to the father we have always wanted and whom we know we should have had. We have to let go of rightful expectations—of our need to be right over being happy. Once we stop waiting for the father we can never have, we will start healing our deepest wound and start being our real selves.

# AT MY FATHER'S WEDDING

## His Legacy

"... On my father's wedding day,
  no one was there
  to hold him. Noble loneliness
  held him. Since he never asked for pity
  his friends thought he
  was whole. Walking alone, he could carry it ..."

  "On My Father's Wedding 1924"
  Robert Bly

No one held my father on his wedding day. He was probably scared on the day he married my mother, and on many days before and after. On that special afternoon, I bet my dad would have liked to have talked to his father honestly about his fears, to have wept with him: "Tell me the secrets of love. Explain the mystery of sex. Tell-me-how-to-be-a-man." But my father was unable to feel his own pain, and he had learned by then to shut out his inner world like most men of his generation and the generations before him.

Because my grandfather did not instruct him on how to

be a man, but merely how to do "manly" things, my father was wounded and he passed on that wound to my brother and me. No one was there to hold my brother at his wedding. And I, having so much fear and little faith in marriage and commitment, and not knowing even how to let someone hold me, was not emotionally or spiritually ready to marry until my fortieth year.

I remember the first time a woman said, "Why don't you ever let me hold you?" I looked at her like she was crazy. It was my job to hold women, for I'd never been shown how to be held by my father, and I'd never seen him being held by my mother. Held *up*, yes, when drunk, but not held gently, lovingly, as if it were natural and okay.

I said I would try. I tried for ten minutes turning my body in every direction, trying to find a position that was comfortable and just a little familiar, contorting and grumbling, "What do I do with this arm?" Finally I found a place beside her, and she held me, and I cried for a long time. It was so hard to be held, so foreign and scary. That woman reminded me of the distance between my dad and me in so many ways.

I remember the first time a man held me while I wept. It felt so odd, so necessary, so long overdue. The weeping that began over feeling the pain of the loss of a love turned into deep grieving for the lack of male support, touch, and tenderness.

I wish my dad could have been held by his dad. I grieve the fact that he wasn't, and that I wasn't. And in that grieving I reduce the need for that sixty-year-old man in Tampa to come hold me now, to be different from the way he is, or to crawl out of the box his culture and alcoholism forced him into.

I wonder what he would have been like if his father had

held him on his wedding day, and if another man had held him on the day his father died. Perhaps Grandfather might not have remained unburied, still alive and criticizing in Dad's head and his dreams even to this day. And perhaps our legacy would have been wholeness instead of the "noble loneliness" so many of us feel.

## THE GRANDFATHER WOUND

Grandfather: A man who made years of mistakes with his own son, and probably abused his son physically as well by stepping on his soul. I remember my father telling me that he hadn't done anything to me that his dad hadn't first done to him. My father said that one Sunday afternoon without so much as blinking an eye, let alone letting a tear fall. "You didn't have it near as bad as I did. I whipped you with a belt. My dad used plow lines on me when I did something wrong."

It had never occurred to me that the grandfather I revered all those years might have been even half as abusive as my father was to me. Granddad seemed so gentle, so kind, so spiritual.

I was thirty-nine before I realized that the beatings he had given to his son with leather straps and switches became Coca-Colas and Dr Peppers bought on hot Alabama summer days for me, his grandson. He could take me for the walks and drives in the country that he could not take his own son on. I was the son he never had, not because Dad couldn't have been, but because Granddad was a young father and didn't know what he knew after letting the years teach him a few things about child rearing. The distance one generation provides allowed my grandfather to behave in ways toward me that may have seemed less than manly for a young man back in the early part of this century. But mostly, I think, it was a factor of time. When you're sixty you tend to believe that you have more time to play with your kids (even though time is running out) or teach them things than you do when you're twenty and struggling to turn time into money so that you can keep food on the table.

Granddaddy was a good grandfather to me. I spent more time by his side than by my own father's. He and I worked together on the land, in his chicken house, and we talked endlessly when I rode with him on the county school-bus he drove for years. Dad and I never spent time talking, and when we worked together he was a hard taskmaster.

Granddad and I watched wrestling on Saturday afternoons long before the men were painted and wore spiked hair and yelled insults at the audience. Dad and I spent most of our Saturday nights yelling at each other and wrestling for my mother's attention. Granddad and I shot rats in the chicken house late at night. Sometimes I wished I could shoot Dad on days that he hurt my mother, sister, brother, and me. Granddad taught me how to say grace and that true spirituality was more important than religion. Dad would drop my sister and me off at church on Sunday mornings and go back home to nurse a hangover while holding on to the belief he learned as a boy in Sunday school, "Once saved always saved."

And when my grandfather died during my thirteenth year, his burial was the backwards ritual of my manhood.

This rite of passage, which so many men experience, came after the funeral when my parents and I went to my grandparents' house to see my grandmother. Before we got there, my dad made it clear that I was to "be a man, think of Grandma, try not to upset her, be strong for her." But when I saw her in the dim light of the darkened bedroom where they used to let me sleep on the foldout couch, I cried, letting everybody down. I was crying for my grandmother, not for my precious dead grandfather, my island of sanity in an otherwise chaotic childhood. I could see how sad she was and how lonely she, like me, would be, without him.

Mom and Dad let me hug her for a split second and then sent me out of the room. I sat out in my parents' car with my cousin, and neither of us shed a tear for the man we loved so much. Six silent men had carried him on their shoulders and put him in the ground, and neither my father nor I wept for the man who had influenced us both. If my dad did cry, he did not let me see, and I became solid in my stoicism, determined not to let my mom and dad down again. I would be a "man" if it killed me.

Not until I was thirty-three years old, twenty years after he died, did I cry about the loss, the tearing away of my grandfather. My grieving was the lost ritual that no one had performed with me or had allowed me to perform myself when I was thirteen. It was a necessary loss and ritual that helped me turn a legacy of pain into wholeness.

## THE LOST RITUAL OF MANHOOD

In primitive cultures, young boys often get wounded in initiation ceremonies: a tooth is knocked out, an incision is made, and a boy becomes a man through a painful ordeal. The pain lasts minutes, hours, maybe a few days, but afterwards the boy has become a man, physically and symbolically in everyone's eyes. American males have no such rituals. They have pain in their daily lives, to be sure, but it is a pain produced from lack of ritual and ceremony. An American boy walks in a man's suit but stays forever a boy, because he never feels certain that he has won the right to enter into the world of men.

Another reason a man stays a boy is because his father never let him win or be right at a critical moment in his development. Robert Bly speaks of the hollow victory a father feels when he shames his son by not letting him win an argument or game. And how the boy feels betrayed but can't say how or why and the defeat follows him like the demon that follows his own dad.

At a certain point in any boy's life, his father should let him win, be right, be victorious. Whether the battle is physical or intellectual, it is symbolic for the boy who would become a man. Perhaps when the father and son are arguing, the father can simply look at the son and say, "You know, you're right. I'm wrong." Or maybe when they're playing a little one-on-one basketball in the driveway, the father can let him win and then tell him what a good game he played.

But most men can't do that. And their fathers couldn't do it for them either. My father always had to be right, stronger, smarter, and wealthier. He had to win because his father never accepted defeat from him. He had to win with me because he was losing to so many other people so much of the time. He couldn't lose to me, too, because he felt that one more slice out of his self-esteem would have killed him.

A son who can never win with his father is forever unsure

of himself. While he resents his father, he still sees him as "the one who knows everything." He projects onto his father a power that he never claims for himself. His dad is a godlike figure who is silently worshipped and not crossed. He always sees his father as a boy sees; even the son standing six feet tall to his dad's five-feet-nine, slightly bent body still sees his father as bigger. And he shrinks in his dad's presence so that though he walked into his father's house a full six feet, by the time he leaves he can barely see over the steering wheel of his car.

Because the son stays a boy in his father's eyes and his own, he never feels equal to the father or ever grown up. He usually becomes arrogant, cocky, and defensive to compensate for his lost manhood, or he becomes angry, or maybe he even becomes passive, soft, silly, and a mamma's boy. The son's confidence in himself is so low that he may raise a son whom he beats in order to feel like a man. He may similarly strive to dominate any woman he encounters.

Because our society does not have set rituals for us to observe, we have to make ourselves conscious of what we and our sons need, we have to create meaning in our daily lives together. If a father is healthy enough to choose to let his son win just once at the right moment, his son will feel full and whole. His victory would be touched with a little sadness because he would feel that he was leaving his boyhood and his father to some subtle degree. His father will also feel some grief, knowing that his boy is growing up as he is growing old. But both will have participated in a truthful moment of manhood, a rightful and graceful passage.

## KILLING THE FATHER

A man turns into a father all at once—no warning, no preparation, no classes. A woman starts turning into a mother in her early childhood. After all, she spends many hours pretending that she's holding a baby, feeding it, changing its diapers, and nurturing it. Her doll is her someday child.

At the dinner table sits a young father who feeds himself and a mother who feeds her living doll; a child, by nature, sucks in all the food and energy the parents can provide. The father feels like there's enough food to go around, but some part of him he can't quite locate feels that he's not getting enough of the woman's energy, time, or attention, as he did before the permanent guest arrived.

He looks at the baby then at the mother, then down at his full plate and feels at the same moment empty and full of shame. Embarrassed by his resentment toward the son he wanted so much, he gets up and walks away and sometimes keeps on walking. Sometimes he just goes to his recliner and sits down and turns on the TV, picks up the paper, and proceeds sullenly to coproduce a boy who wonders why his father wanted him in the first place. Wonders why his dad gets so uptight every time he comes home for a visit. The son wonders one day at work where this driving feeling of competition he and other men constantly carry comes from. He wonders when his father will finally welcome him into the world of men and thank him for appearing on the planet. Both men wonder if men were just meant to use stares, insults, and arguments to split the energy of the mother as if she were some atom capable of energizing them more fully if they could only have her to themselves.

For the answer read *Oedipus* by Sophocles on some rainy

afternoon. This ancient author knew much about the father-son wound. He knew every son must someday "kill the father," which every son knows and every father also knows, which is why it's so difficult for Dad to acknowledge that his son is becoming a man. Where there are two men and one woman, the energy is shared. Where there is a man who knows there is enough energy to go around, the split is seldom seen. Where there is a woman who holds to her own energy and doesn't feel responsible for a man's, men can come and go and leave her still feeling whole and intact. On good days there's plenty of energy to go around.

When a son rejects his father's fears that there is too little energy to go around and asserts himself, he begins to "kill the father" in another necessary rite of passage. If a son finds the courage and responds to the need to look his father squarely in the eyes until the elder looks away, he's done it. When the son finally allows himself to succeed in the areas in which his father failed, then he's accomplished it. The day the son breaks the pattern that has tied him to his father's psyche and soul, he's achieved it. These are just a few of the ways that the son symbolically and necessarily "kills the father."

Each man must find the manner that suits him to kill off the father who lives in his muscles, brain, soul, and dreams. Each man must wrestle with the fear that comes with the process and the ongoing destruction. If a man does not kill his father, the father will know it and on one level be glad to continue being the dad. But on another level, he'll never respect his son who never quite became a man and the equal and perhaps friend he's always longed for his son to be.

"When I go home," said Jason, "Dad's Dad, and I'm like I was at twelve or thirteen. Nothing has changed. When we're sitting around at night talking, he'll get up from his chair and say, 'Well, it's time we all get to bed. We need our rest,' and we all do it, including me." The forty-two-year-old attorney looked not a day over thirty, even though as he talked in the men's group his shoulders curved toward the floor.

Lots of men think that if they have children and become fathers that this will "kill the father," but this alone is not enough. "My dad tells me how to raise my own son and points out ways I'm screwing my boy up every time I go home for a visit," says Roger who is thirty-seven and a licensed child psychologist. Roger doesn't see that his father does this because Roger lets him, doesn't stop him, just gets mad at him, holds it in, and swears he's not going home again, but then returns to experience it all over again.

What happens to the son who kills the father? He confronts his worst fear, which is buried so deep that most men never acknowledge it, that Dad will disappear, reject him, and the son will die. Most men forget that Dad did a lot of disappearing and rejecting all during their earlier years but still they didn't die. The son also confronts another fear, which is his own mortality. For as long as Dad is Dad and he's his son, his boy, then he won't really have to grow up, become responsible for himself (because Dad is still responsible for his life and situation), and finally get old and die. When a son kills his father he becomes a man who will someday be "killed" by his own son. The moment a man kills his father he tastes his own death.

In the poem "Do Not Go Gentle Into That Good Night" by Dylan Thomas, the speaker is watching his father die and he demands his father, "Rage, rage against the dying of the light . . . Do not go gentle into that good night." In other words, whether Dad is dying physically or in a son's psyche, the son faces his own death at that moment.

When a son metaphorically kills his father, he will have more energy. He'll get more things done than he would have if Dad's voice had been pushing him in other directions. He'd be more likely to act on Joseph Campbell's injunction, "Follow your bliss." He'd take back the projection of godliness he'd placed on his father, see him as "simply" human, and become more human himself. He'd stop making other men and women into the parent who wasn't there for him. He'd become an anchor to his own children and a model for masculinity and an adult when he's with his lover or wife. The son who kills the father becomes a man and stops being a boy.

# FATHERS WHO TAUGHT US NOT TO GRIEVE, GIVE, OR RECEIVE

R emember watching your dad shave? Perhaps you put some of his thick white cream all over your face and then with the smooth side of a comb sliced it off as he removed his whiskers as well as your doubts about whose boy you really were. Now you look in the mirror or watch the way you talk to your kids, your dog, your wife, or your lover and you still see whose boy you are.

The patterns that we share with our fathers and the patterns we develop in reaction to theirs are often our only connection to them.

If Dad drank Jack Daniels whiskey twice a day, we take a couple of pulls off a Jim Bean bottle (we won't drink the same brand because that would be admitting he knew which was better). If Dad raged and we rage, we feel a little closer to him than if we were to stay stoic and silent. If Dad's first love was his work, we take our job to be our full-time mistress and wonder if Dad is watching from his grave as we work ourselves into an early one.

Many sons share their fathers' patterns, others purposely develop opposite thoughts and behaviors that can be used to get back at Pop for not performing the role of father adequately enough to suit the son. Little acts of rebellion show our resentment—Dad wears his hair short and is clean-shaven; the son wears his long and sports a full beard. Bigger ones—if Dad was obsessive about money, the son creates a carefree lifestyle of throwing his money away, and lives out his father's worst fear—running out of money.

Some men's fathers were so successful that the sons create a life where they—consciously or unconsciously— never quite succeed. Other sons who watched their fathers fail make sure they themselves never succeed by sabotaging their efforts so that Dad won't feel so defeated and shamed by his son's success. This son fears that if his father were to feel less a man than his son, he might like his son even less. But more likely, the son is so pissed off at his father that he doesn't want to give his dad the satisfaction of seeing him succeed because he might sit back one day on lunch break with his buddies at the plant and claim credit for his son's accomplishments.

Dad didn't get his financial life in order; neither does the son. Pop couldn't make a relationship work; neither can the son. Two peas in a pod. Opposites at work: Dad was a construction worker, the son becomes a lawyer. Dad was an alcoholic, the son uses drugs or becomes a preacher. Dad yelled and screamed when he was angry; the son holds in his anger and lets it ooze out in passive-aggressive ways. The desire for a connection to the father is further indicated in the way we choose to father our children based on our unconscious selection of the dysfunctional fathering styles we saw and imitated or reacted to.

What follows are a number of different styles of fathering with which most men can identify. You may have absorbed only one style because this was the predominant way your father fathered you. Chances are, though, you may recognize several, since most fathers are a complex composition of their own fathers, uncles, grandfathers, and other important men in their past.

The first fathering style is The Man Who Would Be King: This dad believed that since he worked hard all day (for the real King—Money), when he returned home his children and wife should act like loyal subjects. "Don't bother Daddy. He's working hard for us," says not the queen but the head servant. This father ruled his kingdom from a La-Z-Boy recliner, sometimes granting pardons, but more often performing the role of principal punisher and executioner. He was the old "wait-until-your-father-gets-home" dad. What he said was the law of the land because he owned the roof over your head.

My dad had an overdeveloped attachment to his roof. He talked about his roof a lot, and referred to it constantly when I dared question the King's decree for me. "This is my house. You live under my roof. As long as you are under this roof, you'll do as you're told. When you get your own roof you can do whatever you want to, but while you're under my roof you'll do what I say when I say it." Damn, I thought to myself. I can't wait to get my own roof.

The second style is the Critical Father: This father was full of negative criticism, frustration, and anger. No one could ever do anything right enough or on time enough to please him. He'd find a flaw in every thought, word, or deed. "You can do better than that, can't you?" "What's wrong with you? Are you stupid?" "You'll never amount to anything." "If I've shown you once I've shown you a thousand times. Get out of the way. I might as well do it myself." "Can't you do anything right?" His perfectionism and criticism pricked us and him everyday.

The Passive Father gave over all duties, responsibilities, and power to the mother, the children, the boss, the society, the government, or some combination of these. Truly a pawn, he was moved by some greater will than his own. He didn't interact, interrupt, intercede, or show any interest. He was there but not really. Occasionally he'd take a risk and offer a suggestion or a comment or provide some defense of himself or us only to be beaten down, or ignored. He silently crawled into books, booze, or TV or grew too fond of his garden or study while his son grew up hating passivity of any kind whether in men, women, or his own children.

The Absentee Father: Much like the passive dad, he wasn't there for his son. He disappeared at dawn and wouldn't return until late at night. He might be encountered once at the refrigerator on the night both of you got hungry at the same time. You may have bumped into him as you both stumbled in the dark. The meeting was cordial, though slightly cool. And by the next morning you weren't sure if you really had run into him or if it had been just a nightmare. This dad wasn't there for the ball games or the recitals you played in. He wasn't at your graduation—he was too busy. He wasn't there to tell you about your penis; Mom had to do that. He wasn't there to tell you about sex; Mom couldn't do that. Hell, he wasn't there emotionally when he helped conceive you and he wasn't there when you were born.

These fathering styles wound the son. The son assimi-
lates these styles and either reproduces or rebels against
them. The son raised by the absentee father may smother
his son or daughter and be unable to let his child grow up.
The passive father might raise a son who becomes so active
in politics, bureaucracy, work, relationships that he can't
slow down and let his wife or coworkers take their fair share
of responsibility for making things happen. The passively
raised son may become the Man-Who-Would-Be-King
kind of father almost as if to show his dad how a real despot
would manage things. More likely, though, the passively
raised son will find himself acting like his father in ways
he hated as a child, and hates to see in himself, but feels
powerless to change.

The critical father produces a son who sees himself as
never being good enough or worthy of love, success, time,
attention, praise, or tenderness. He keeps working and
waiting for someone to tell him he's good enough at last,
to take it easy and not push so hard. He finds his main talent
lies in observing what his wife, children, employees,
friends, and relatives are doing wrong. He waits for someone to tell him they're proud of him, but when they do he
can't hear it or it just doesn't count as much as it would
have if his dad had said it and meant it when he was seven
or ten or fourteen. He might allow himself to be criticized
by bosses, wives, and friends. He might even let people he
does not know cut him to pieces, believing they're doing it
for "his own good" or because they "love" him.

The Father Who Would Be King usually raises a son who
says the same things his father said to him about roofs and
obedience. His word is law and he thinks he knows everything.

There standing in that mirror today is a man shaving his father's face, a man who would rather be right than happy. There stands a man yelling at his kids in a way that surprises and confuses him, because as a boy he said he'd never do this if he ever had kids. Or there you sit in your La-Z-Boy recliner letting the family run itself. Or perhaps you are more like me, and worked hard to be the opposite of everything Dad was externally, only to run smack into him again and again in the really deep ways.

My own healing process has needed lots of time, lots of work, lots of acceptance of the many sides of me and my father that I have wanted to deny. It has also taken a while to heal some of the wounds I received and to forgive myself for some of the same wounds I've inflicted. But recognizing your father's style of parenting, becoming conscious of the patterns you share with your father, or the ways in which you have made yourself purposely different is a first step in finding your father, separating from him, and reclaiming your life as your own.

## MEN GIVING AND RECEIVING: KEEPING SCORE

It's hard to believe that in the little time my dad and I spent together, I learned so many things that I wish I hadn't. I became like him in many ways. One thing I learned was the inability to let people give to me. My father could demand, expect, and extract, but neither he nor I (until recently) could just receive. This inability has cost us both a great deal.

Look most men in the eyes and tell them, "I want to give you this." No matter what the gift is, the giver will be suspect and questioned silently—or perhaps loudly—about his motives: "What do you want from me?" "How much will this cost later?" "Confess. What are you really after?" Most men grew up believing no one gets something for nothing in this world. And though many of us were taught never to look a gift horse in the mouth, we usually stare into the giver's face to see if we can get a clue as to why they're giving us something for nothing.

Why are so many men so unable to receive? One reason is that as children our parents or uncles or grandparents usually gave with strings attached and hooks that would be used later to catch us and reel us in like fish floundering on deck. Each person kept a mental record of how much they gave and more importantly, how much they were owed.

When I was a teenager my father would give me money and later try to shame me or guilt me into doing what he wanted. I would receive a dollar, and he'd exact a pound of flesh.

"Come on out to the garden and help me," he'd say on Sundays after dinner.

"No thanks, Dad, I'm tired. I just want to talk or watch TV."

He'd storm outside uttering the words sure to shame. "Well, don't come around me next week asking for more money if you can't give me a hand from time to time."

I would always wish I hadn't taken a cent from him and vow never to do so again.

There is a side to this that I've only recently uncovered, and it's important to our understanding of our fathers. I believe my dad gave to me with hooks firmly in place because he wanted to be with me and he didn't know how to ask straight out. He couldn't say, "I want to spend time with you. I miss seeing you. I want to be close. Come out to the garden and break the solitude I surround myself with. Please, son, break the monotony of the constant chatting I do with myself when you're not near."

He couldn't say it, so he unconsciously conspired to keep me indebted to him. Because so many men had fathers and mothers, or perhaps grandparents who were afraid to give unconditionally, they learned to suspect kindness that asks no payment in return.

The first time a woman offered to make love to me and said that I was just to "relax and receive," I thought she had to have an agenda and that I'd pay later. What could she want? I was so stunned and confused that I spent our time together hiding in my head and analyzing her motives instead of feeling the pleasure of being with her, missing the moment, confusing her intentions with my father's.

During the early part of my recovery from my traumatic childhood as an adult child of an alcoholic, I got in touch with how I couldn't receive gracefully. I could give—not gracefully, mind you—but I did give a lot of myself, my time, my money, even to the point of doing without on occasion— sacrificing till it hurt. It was years before I realized that a lot of my giving was rooted in the hope that someday someone would give to me. The catch was, when someone would try to give I wouldn't let them because I couldn't let it in.

More recently I realized that my way of giving was more like my father's than I had ever cared to admit. In the past I have given several women money to help them move closer to me, which eventually resulted in their moving farther away emotionally, if not geographically. Or I've just "loaned" them money to help them out. But deep down inside I always expected them to pay me back, not in monetary terms, but in service, silence, or sex.

Only in recent years have I been able to give and not expect to get. And recently I have begun to trust that some people really have my best interests at heart. When they want to give, I try to let them.

I've come to believe that until a man can receive, it will be impossible for him truly to give, without hooks and strings. Until we learn that everyone we encounter, need, and love is not going to act as our parents did, we'll miss that which can nurture us most—and which we don't have to pay for: smiles, massages, hugs, and most important of all, love.

## ACCEPTING THE ABSENT FATHER

You probably don't remember this scene: Dad standing in the bedroom doorway, almost as tall as the door itself. With a scowl on his face and one hand slicing the air that is thick with tension, he looks at your mother and you in her arms crying your lungs out, and says, "Can't you keep him quiet? He cries all of the time. Shut him up, will you?" His tone scares you and the woman he "loves."

Another scene you may remember: At six you fall off your bike and cut your leg badly. You stumble into the house, crying. The tears, the snot, and the blood get only this response from Dad: "Stop crying and tell me what happened. You're a big boy. You'll be all right. You're not that hurt. Now stop crying, damn it, or I'll really give you something to cry about." You stop. You don't cry again until you're thirty—or at least not when anyone can see you. Sure, you may cry at sad movies under the cover of darkness. But do you ever weep for your own life, your own

28

lost childhood? Not on your worst day, not with your best friend, certainly not in front of your wife or kids and most assuredly not in front of any man.

You may remember yourself at fifteen. You were fat, or perhaps skinny, certainly pimple-faced and scared. You and your dad started talking about your grades, about your hair, about your clothes, about your friends. "Dad, you never listen to me. You never *have* listened to me." And he said something like, "That's crap. I don't know what you want from me. Tell me, what do you want? And take that goddamn earring out of your ear while you're in my house." You looked at him and wondered if there had ever been any love between you and him, him and your mom, him and his dad, him and his mom. And you shouted so loud that fathers all over the world should have been able to hear if they had just been listening, "I just want you to listen to me. I want you to try just once to understand me. Understand how I feel, goddammit." But all you got was, "Boy, you can't talk to me that way in my own house."

You moved out of your father's house and into a distant silence. You became spiritually and emotionally homeless and never wanted to talk about your losses, of your father, or the loss of your own voice.

Twenty years later, you still may not talk to anyone. You hold everything in, trusting no one. You believe no one can really listen, really understand you. You don't know your father, don't much like him, but still argue with him every time you visit your father's house. Your father still doesn't know you, but still believes he knows what's best for you.

Perhaps this is one reason why, when a son finally shows up at a men's group or gathering or even a Twelve-Step support group and sees people talking and sharing their pain and their healing process, he feels like an intruder, feels as if he doesn't belong there. He feels awkward, and scared. He's unable to believe his own eyes and ears, which tell him that he *can* be heard.

A father who does not listen, hear, or understand his son wounds him in the same way his father wounded him. At a deep level, the father may even recognize the familiarity of it all. His son, for lack of a positive example, has never learned how to listen, so the father has never been heard either. Fathers want to be understood and heard just as much as any son. And fathers especially want to be heard by their own sons. But the son who is not first heard by his father listens and speaks to no one, not even himself.

When a son does speak finally about his father, he may look up at the ceiling, into the sky, and away from his wounded soul, as he says, "I think Dad did the best he could. He worked real hard. He was a good provider. Sure, he made some mistakes, but he wasn't any worse than anybody else's father. . . . So I don't really see why we need to spend time talking about him. He was never there. It's my mom that I need to deal with. I got lots of stuff about her. I'm pretty sure she's the reason my relationships are so screwed up." The speed with which the son steers the conversation away from the father and toward the mother is both telling and natural.

Many men feel much freer to deal with their emotions about their mothers simply because they were more present and available and therefore observable. It's easier for us to see their flaws and faults and how they affected us. Dad, on the other hand, is a mystery, a figure who crept in and out in the dark after we went to bed and before we got up. Most men didn't see their fathers enough to know for sure what personality traits they inherited from them and what they picked up from their brief encounters with the milkman and the mailman.

Mom is the safer parent to work on for a number of reasons. Sometimes, I ask a man at a men's group to fill in the blank after this phrase: "Mom will always_____." Eight out of ten respond something like this: "Mom will always *be there*, or *love me*, or *accept me*." If I ask men to fill in the blank after the phrase: "Dad will always_____," the same eight out of ten men will reply, "Dad will always *criticize me*, *leave me*, *hurt me*, *abandon me*, or *yell at me*." Men are afraid that if they start to feel their feelings about their dad, he won't be there at the end of the process— especially since most fathers weren't there at the beginning.

Another reason it's safer to work on Mother issues is that our connection to her is usually ropelike, where our connection to our father is tenuous, more like a spider's thread. We are afraid that if we start working on him, the slender connection we have will be severed once and for all, and we'll float out into space, no longer anchored to our only model, our first model (however toxic or flawed) of masculinity. A little boy in us feels that he will never be fathered at all if he lets go of the only father he ever had. Who will take care of us, provide a roof over our heads, and put food for our stomachs, if not Dad? If we make him angry, he could leave us to die alone.

Dad somehow delivered the message to us that if we were to demonstrate our sadness or anger, he would be greatly disappointed in us because in his opinion, sharing emotion is not manly. So we don't want to confront him or his inadequacies, even if he can't see or hear us, even in the safety of a men's group. We don't want to feel our pain even at a

Twelve-Step meeting. So we put off feeling our pain, venting our anger, so that our wounds can't heal until the last possible moment. We wait and wait for Dad to come through for us—we wait until the second or third divorce, or until we have broken up with someone we loved more than we could say or show or feel. Then we can't deny anymore how hopeless our expectations are, how fruitless our waiting is. But if we accept that our fathers will always be distant, absent, we can begin to acknowledge our pain and gently probe and clean the wound—by ourselves and in the company of other men.

## AT A MEN'S MEETING:
## FIGHTING, LOVING, AND LEAVING THE FATHER

Off a main road onto a trail worn down by years of tractors and trucks lies Marvin Allen's grandfather's West Texas ranch where Marvin, the director of the Texas Men's Center, and I have led several men's retreats. Toyotas, Volvos, and Lincolns always look out of place as they cross the rugged landscape of mesquite, cactus, and cow piles to get to the meeting site as they were doing on a recent Saturday morning.

About one hundred and fifty men were attending this men's gathering. They'd come for a three-day camp-out and inner journey that would bring them face-to-face with their fears, their fathers, their failures, and each other. They had fanned out over three or four acres to find their spot, put up their tent, and store their gear. Many looked hesitant, unsure of the harsh West Texas terrain, questioning their motives for being there.

Friday night and Saturday morning were full of feelings and fears. Groups of men talked and beat drums and shared to put men at ease with each other, while they did some of the deepest emotional work they ever had done.

By Saturday afternoon it was hot and the sun looked as tired as the men whom it had been heating all day. I was leading a group in which a young man named Chris had begun talking. Chris stood a well-built six feet tall, every muscle on him gained from doing construction work in Florida. He was full of anger. In spite of his physical strength, his face looked worn and beaten though not quite defeated. "I'm tired of holding this anger in me and I'm getting ready to tell my dad how I really feel." All the men paid close attention to Chris since he was speaking for most of them, too.

Chris was like a lot of men I work with and he's a lot like me. I used to be very angry at my dad. Like Chris, I wanted to tell him how I felt, but for decades I was too afraid of how he would react. Chris, too, was afraid of his dad's reaction, afraid that he would either act hurt and sulk away in silence or go into a rage and hit him the way he had when Chris was a child. Chris was so full of fear that every time he was with his father he got numb from the neck down.

"I have so much anger in me that it feels like that's all I've got and I know that's not so. I love my dad, but I'm so angry that I don't feel anything else for him." Chris wept while he spoke. "I don't know where to begin or what to say, or even if I should say anything to him at all. But this anger has been eating me up inside for years. I've wanted to confront him and have this stuff healed up by this Father's Day, but I see that's an artificial deadline I've placed on myself." A man nearby held out his hand and Chris grabbed it desperately and thankfully. "I know it's not going to change overnight, but sometimes I think I'll never be any different. We still fight and argue and end up shouting at each other and calling each other names, just as we have since I was a kid. I never really tell him how I feel—how I've felt for a long time. Sometimes I think anger is all that we have between us. You take that away and we wouldn't have anything. And I'm real scared to say this. You know what scares me the most? The fear that one day I'll figure out how to talk to him and tell him how I feel, and he'll listen and even apologize to me and tell me he really understands my feelings. You guys may think I'm crazy, but that scares me to death."

Now Chris was sobbing, as were most of the other men in the crowd. "I know how to fight with my dad, but I don't know how to just love him."

Chris was in the kind of pain that many men understand. He had begun to realize that ignoring his problems with his father was deadening his feelings inside and out. And he was trying to find a way out of the waiting game he was playing with his father, a way to break out of the bleak, destructive pattern and scenarios of men's predictable fights. And yet he felt the risk that change presented for him—although he hated their relationship, he had not yet found the healing path that would lead him out of their almost compulsive tearing at each other's wounds and into a positive relationship. Their acts toward each other had become so rigid that Chris needed to learn new behaviors, new ways of relating. And this new territory scared him, but it would also lead to his, and maybe his father's, healing. These feelings were the beginning of leaving behind false and hurtful expectations and of enabling his knowing his father and himself.

## AT ANOTHER MEN'S MEETING:
## SEEING OUR FATHERS WITH OUR OWN EYES

Fog clung to the mountains of New Mexico that overlook Las Vegas, a small town seventy miles outside of Santa Fe. Rain met the men as they moved from their cars to tents, to the barn where we huddled, worked on ourselves, and waited for the sky to clear so we could go back to the site cleared for the one hundred and thirty men who attended the gathering led by Marvin Allen, Shepherd Bliss, and me.

Dave, an artist with small hands, round face, and tense brown eyes reminded me of Chris from the last gathering because he held in him as much sadness as Chris stored anger, the sibling of sadness.

More than once Dave started to cry and then stopped as his feelings stalled out and were submerged as he flew away from his past and his pain. He tried to explain in a logical way what was going wrong in his life so we'd understand, but his voice lacked feeling. He talked about how he'd done some reconnecting with the little boy inside who had been hurt, and he felt good about the work he had done. He had even begun to forgive the adolescent who had acted out and "jerked everybody around and jerked off." Now he needed some attention and some healing. That was why he had come. He said he couldn't contain the emotions any longer.

All of a sudden in the middle of his dry description the tears started to flow. "I missed knowing my dad. My mom told me how I should feel about my father. I saw him through her eyes and I never got to see him with my own. And now he's dead and it's too late. I miss him so much. He used to let me work with him sometimes, and the things he helped me build are the only things I remember complet-

35

ing as a teenager. I can't seem to complete anything now."

He cried, and all the men who were understanding and feeling every word in their bodies came over to him and wrapped him with their arms. They held him as he sobbed for a father who he never really saw, never really knew.

Robert Bly tells a story about a man who went in search of a father who had left him and his mother when he was very young. What he knew, what he believed and hated about his father had been largely planted in his head by his mother. Then, in his thirties, the man found himself on his father's doorstep, ringing a doorbell, watching a door open, wondering what his father would say. Would it be, "Go away, get out of here. Leave me alone"? I'm sure this was his worst fear. The old man came to the door and recognized his son. The young man said, "I've come to get to know you, to see you, and make my own decision about who you are and who you aren't. I don't want to see you through my mother's eyes any longer." The old man looked at his son and said, "Now I can die in peace."

Today, as I sit and write about men, myself, and my father, I wonder if my dad missed seeing me with his own eyes. He was gone so much of the time that he must have had to rely on what Mother said about me late at night when he'd come home from work. I wonder if he missed telling me stories, holding me in his lap, seeing me grow. I wonder if he'd have liked to have been around me more and gotten to know me the way you can only know someone by pitching a ball to him or going fishing. We tried to do these things on a couple of occasions without much success. When we were out in the front yard throwing to each other, his attention seemed to be somewhere else, and when I couldn't catch the ball with the competency he expected, he quickly became impatient and went back into the house. Similarly, when we went fishing, I got my line all tangled up and he ended up snapping at me, and further ugliness that I don't remember made me go into shock. I still don't like to fish.

I wonder if our relationship would have improved if we had time to settle into each other's ways a bit more and practice putting our personalities and bodies against each other.

By feeling every ounce and pound and ton of grief and anger I felt at not getting to see my dad, be with my dad, and wishing that my dad wanted to be with me, I got closer to seeing him as he really was and really is.

The hours spent pounding a pillow, pressing a pencil hard into a journal, and screaming out in anguish, not to mention the work in therapy and Twelve-Step groups started paying off. My back straightened and I got better. My face relaxed and I became lighter. My anger was discharged and I became more responsible for my own life. I didn't know it then, but I was well on my way to letting the dad I never had go and getting ready to see him and me as more human than ever before.

This is what I hope you will gain from the encounters with the raw emotions of Chris and Dave, and the other men in our gatherings—a knowledge of your own deep woundedness and a knowledge that feeling this long-denied pain can be the route to a new appreciation of yourself and mastery over your life.


## FATHERS GIVING TIME

A childless, would-be father, I walk in the evening as the sun turns everything it touches into a shade of gold, catching anything that moves, flies, or stands still and making it pleasing to the eye. At this time of day, I miss children the most and I watch and listen with greedy eyes and ears to the laughter, stories, and tears of other men's children. Some days when I watch the way fathers let their children's smiles go unnoticed, their scratches unkissed, and their voices unheard, I want to run over to the father and simply say, "Please pay attention."

When I hear the words "baby" or "child," a part of me wants to cry out for comfort. Because I never had a childhood, instead of filling me with hope for the future and warmth for the past, these words simply mean loss.

Today, I heard a boy throw a stick against the ground and say, "Listen, Daddy, to the sound I make with this stick." The daddy kept walking and told his son to hurry up or he was going to leave him. Later I saw a small, round-faced girl pick up a rock as her daddy window-shopped through his busy mind, looking at all he did or didn't do that day or in his lifetime, or perhaps he was thinking of all he could buy if he just knew how to turn lead into gold. She held the rock up to him; she was as excited as if it were the gold that he longed for. "Put that dirty thing down, young lady. It's nasty." She put it down, and something in her face and perhaps her soul disappeared. God in a rock held up by two small hands became something nasty, and she might never feel and see a stone again. When she grows up like her daddy and me, will she tell her child to put God down in favor of window-shopping? When she grows up to be as big as her daddy, will she tell her child to put God down in favor of window-shopping, too? And will she feel far away from herself and those she loves on days when rocks could still be sacred and sticks could still make music?

If we men would slow down long enough to feel the loss of our childhoods and grieve over the words "baby" and "child," if we would let ourselves weep over the fact that someone hurried us when we needed to be seen, heard, and perhaps indulged a bit, I have to believe we'd feel closer to ourselves, and we just might be able to become the fathers we never had.

# MAN WITHOUT MAN

## How the Wound Keeps Men Apart from Each Other and Themselves

Most men are afraid to trust each other. Although they may have difficulties relating to women and may even be to varying degrees woman-hating (having learned our society's lessons well), they trust women more than they trust other men.

Many men feel they have more reasons not to be friends with men than they have men friends. One such reason to stand apart from other men is: If your father couldn't be there for you, then how is this guy you just met going to be there? If your dad, uncles, big brothers, or grandfathers were abusive, shaming, or always abandoning you for work, whiskey, or women, how do you ever build trust for other men?

Put simply, men were taught in their boyhood not to trust other men. Here's one perfect example of this recounted in an article by writer and workshop leader Jed Diamond in *MAN!* magazine:

> "I remember the day it happened, clear as if it was yesterday," Robert said. His expression didn't change. Only something deep in his eyes revealed his feelings. "I yelled out, 'Daddy, Daddy,' as I jumped off the kitchen chair and flew through the air with my arms outstretched. But just as I reached out to him, he turned away and I hit my head on the table as I fell to the floor. I don't remember much after that, except Dad yelling at me to be quiet as we drove to the hospital. Days later . . ." Robert's gaze was steady as he remembered his father's words. I couldn't hold back the tears that ran down my own cheeks when he continued. "Dad took me on his lap and said, 'Baby boy, you have to learn—you can't trust anyone in this life, not even your own father.'"

If you ask a man about his men friends before he begins his recovery, or before he attends a men's gathering, he'll often reply something like, "Well, yeah, I got men friends, sure I do. Me and this guy Joe have been friends for twenty years. He's my best friend. The only problem is he moved across the country about ten years ago. We still talk and get together when we can. I can tell Joe anything. But I can't seem to find guys here like Joe." I say, bullshit—this man's afraid to trust again. After all, Joe left him, too, just as his father likely did, either once or over and over again.

When men don't seek out other men to be their friends, they will most likely turn to women to have all their needs met. Hence, women are asked to bear the burden of men's fear of men. It's my professional opinion and personal experience that this burden is too heavy and is not at all meant for women to carry.

Many women are now refusing to play this role, having done so through many relationships and having watched their moms be their dads' dumping ground and only buddy for years before that. Robert Bly tells a wonderful story about a man who kept bringing all his problems and disappointments to his woman friend. For years she listened and gave well-intentioned advice and probably felt depleted and used at best. Finally, she must have attended a few women's meetings. He arrived to unload his week's worth of garbage and she said something like, "Have you told this to another man?" He, man-friendless of course, had not. "Tell it to another man first and then I'll listen," she said to his shocked face.

Women who do take on what should be shared with men become old women before their time—their shoulders start sagging, their hair graying.

Last year, during a men's conference in Phoenix, a man named Jim shared something he hadn't yet told another man. He stood straight and had shoulders broad enough to make any father proud and any mother comfortable that he could carry any pain she couldn't handle. The gray in Jim's beard at thirty-eight showed he'd been carrying a lot of people's feelings for a long time—as well as his own. "I'm afraid I'm losing my business and that if something doesn't turn around soon I'm going to have to file for bankruptcy." He paused and choked back a tear.

"The only person I've told is my wife, and she's so worried that I can't show her how worried I really am." Now his lips were trembling with fear and emotion. Jim's inability to tell his secret to another man had undoubtedly made his wife's burden even heavier. She not only felt her own fear, but she alone had to be his support, while carrying the weight of his unexpressed worry as well. A few of us in the group shared this insight with Jim, and he wept and then smiled. His burden—and hers—was now a little lighter, and ours was no heavier for the hearing. And we were now united by a common trust, which we all hoped would act as a healing balm on our father-wounds to enable us to develop more and deeper trust of our fellowmen.

## IF YOU CAN'T TRUST YOUR OWN FATHER?

Since we didn't trust our fathers and they didn't trust us, it's difficult for us to trust any man fully. If you did not trust your father in general, then you can't trust him as a masculine role model. Consequently, you can't trust yourself and your masculinity. In simple terms, if you're a man and you perceive your dad to be a competitor, an abuser, or an asshole, and he's your first encounter with manliness, the alpha and omega of masculinity, the Zeus of all that's male—you take it into yourself that you must be a competitor, an abuser, or an asshole.

So if a man can't trust anyone with a cock to be caring, compassionate, and considerate, he looks toward the other gender for this emotional support and for models of behavior. The mother is more available, softer, and will even listen to him sometimes. He turns to the feminine for comfort, nurturing, understanding, and love, and makes his life circle around women, always watching and valuing their every word, gesture, and movement, which he may imitate later, which then usually attracts other women (like his mother) to him.

Turning his back on the meanness he equates with maleness, he comes to overvalue the feminine at the expense of his own masculinity. His appreciation of women, however, is hollow, empty, and immature. This inadequate identity shows in how he treats women, himself, and the planet.

His overdeveloped drive to get in touch with his feminine side looks good to women, confuses men, and keeps him from really being a friend to either sex. He doesn't trust either his feminine side or his maleness, so he becomes what Bly refers to as a "soft male," a man with good intentions, who doesn't want to harm anyone or the planet but who ends up hurting nearly everyone he touches, including himself. He is dangerous because he's gotten in touch with what I call the "false feminine," false because any true and deep contact with that part of himself must first be grounded in the acceptance of himself as a man.

This "soft male" who makes a show of his "false feminine" is easily detectable. He lacks potency in his voice, actions, and being. And while he may love the planet and eat only vegetables, he lacks the ability to take firm action to save the planet or anyone or anything else. He lacks an energy that says "yes" to life and "no" to drugs, alcohol, and other addictions and destructive behaviors.

The son must find the father in order to feel his own masculinity. The father-wound must be opened, descended into, and dealt with in order that he may someday trust his own maleness. Without a deep trust of our own masculinity we will "need" women so much that they will become our souls' sustenance and the center of our universe and we will never understand our own nature, or learn to trust ourselves or other men with our secrets or our lives.

## THE FORGOTTEN BODY: ONE BIG WOUND

If you received shame, or an injury like a whipping or beating, or an icy cold, unresponsive stare from a father's silent face—as a child you probably went numb from the neck down. Any boy subjected to such abuse will try to disappear and will usually fly up into his head, where he'll hide till it's safe to come out. Abuse after abuse leads to his forming intellectual and psychological armor against emotions, against feelings. By detaching from his body he avoids feeling the whipping or the shame. Detaching from the body is the way most of us survived our childhoods.

Frozen inside, we peer out and look at the people walking up to us to be loved or just to give love. Most people use the body to express love, but we can't feel ours for fear the emotions that we carry will overwhelm us and others around us.

Two bodies move close to each other, but a man who has been hurt steers his body from behind his eyes. He stops breathing when love is near. Those who "loved" him were those he most feared; they were the ones who threw everything at him from criticism to cheap china to punches.

He holds in his breath until the pain stops. But the pain never really stops until we let ourselves breathe, until we decide it's safe enough to let down our guard and give our hypervigilance a rest. We hold our bodies up more by our will, rigidity, and fear than by our bones, muscles, and spinal cord.

The wounded man, when told to relax and rest, looks at you as if you're crazy—knowing that you don't understand. When told to let out his anger, rage, and sadness, he points to his body and says, "I can't feel a thing."

Look around and you'll see this deadening process everywhere. A little boy, still in touch with his body, looks at his father as if he were a god. But after the boy has been whipped, slapped, criticized, or shamed into abandoning his body, the god becomes an enemy to be avoided and longed for at the same time.

While a man wants to feel, he knows that if he does he'll hurt. Didn't he learn to leave his body so he wouldn't have to feel pain? But unless we increase our ability to feel the body, we will not be able to give or receive any emotion of real value. We have to become physically conscious again in order to be mentally and emotionally present for ourselves and those we love. We have to learn to trust our bodies, our feelings, and ourselves before we can connect with other men and women.

# MEN, MONEY, AND SEX

W|hen men meet, two subjects will almost always be left out of their conversation: sex and money. Men long to know more about these topics, to know how other men feel, but they are afraid to ask. These two issues make men feel the most vulnerable.

Some men still try to express themselves through John-Wayne–style macho talk about who they have "laid" or how often they "score." But neither they nor men who are working to change themselves can readily talk about their sexual secrets, their performance anxieties, their strengths, and least of all, how it feels to express love through sexual touch and encounter. They are all silent on these subjects.

Most of us men got such little instruction on the art of lovemaking that we try hard not to let anyone see just how little we know, understand, or feel. Our fathers told us little because they probably knew even less than we, as products of the sexual revolution of the sixties, learned from our peers. What they did tell us, we couldn't use. For instance, my father instructed me "to sow my wild oats before I got married and not get anyone pregnant." End of my sexual education from Dad.

So when men get together, "sex" seldom enters the conversation. I hope men can start sharing their secrets about this subject soon. Many of us are worrying ourselves to death because of a lack of information, and we're expecting more from ourselves and our lovers than is reasonable or healthy.

It's important for us to be able to say to our partners that sometimes we're scared and don't feel like making love. Sometimes I just want to be held or touched nonsexually. Sometimes I try so hard to please that "I" get lost in the process. Sometimes I feel guilty when my lover doesn't have an orgasm or as great a one as I had. Sometimes I look at a woman's body and feel inferior faced with such complex, mysterious genitalia. Sometimes I am healthy enough not to take responsibility for my lover's orgasm. Sometimes I want to. Sometimes I can go for weeks or months and not have a sexual need move through my body or mind. Some days I want to make love two or three times. Every once in a while, more and more often, I thank God for my cock and two balls, even the one that hangs lower than the other. And I'm thankful that I'm a man and that I'm learning to listen to the wisdom of my penis. I'm listening to it before placing it in dangerous partners. I'm letting it tell me I'm feeling safe enough for it to be erect.

Besides sex, most men don't feel safe enough to discuss money either. So our money is in the safe deposit box of our minds or locked away in a vault of fear. Men will say things like, "I'm making six figures," or "I'm broke," but when asked how much money they have in their pockets at the moment or in their bank account, they'll usually say, "Enough." I learned in childhood that money is one of, if not the most, important things in life to get and keep. Like many, I was taught: make as much as you can; give as little to the government as you have to; don't tell anyone what you've got, it ain't nobody's business; use it to buy love and affection, and withdraw it from those you want to punish.

For many men, money is a mystery that makes sex seem simple. But most of us think it's very important to act like we know all about it—the interest it makes, how to compound it, what money-market funds and tax-free municipals are. These are things only bankers and accountants really know, and even they are confused about their various complexities.

In large part, men are afraid that there's not enough money to go around, especially if their parents were children of the Great Depression. Many men were taught that once you get some, you better hope it comes with handles so you can hold onto it. Others have such a low regard for "filthy lucre" that they leave it lying around or give it away compulsively. I've worked with more than a few who just plain refuse to make as much money as they can; they want to pay their parents back for giving money such value in the first place. Some men punish their parents by purposely never becoming financially successful so they can silently say, "See what a lousy job of child raising you did. I can't make it." Or, their message might be, "If I make a lot of money, you'll be proud of me and I've wanted you to be proud of me, not my money."

The bottom line is that many men are afraid that if you know how much money they have, you'll have control and power over them, and that if you know their sexual secrets, fears, and failures, you'll really have them by the balls. And with both pieces of information you might try to take everything they have, everything that makes them who they are.

I hope men can learn to trust each other enough to tell how afraid we are, how little we know and how hurt we are around these two subjects. If we don't, we'll expect women to provide us with the emotional support we need to explore these issues and they (for the most part) were not raised to place the same value on money or sex. Many women saw their fathers providing security for their mothers and them as little girls. They gave their fathers their loyalty and otherwise stayed out of their way. They came to understand that in exchange for security, their mothers gave their fathers sex. How can a woman who has learned to measure her self-worth by only relating to a man sexually, hear us and understand? And how can boys who grew up believing the only measure of their worth was the dollars they could accumulate, relate to women?

Add to this the shame women have for trading sex for security. And the shame men carry for not knowing that sex and intimacy are not the same. It's a wonder we relate to each other at all.

So a man must look for understanding from someone who knows and feels the pressure that comes from being the sole provider. Even men who live with women who contribute equally or an even larger paycheck to the family's finances are still afraid that money is the true measure of their masculinity.

So a man and a woman lie quietly next to each other after

having silently traded sex for money (security). And the man doesn't understand why the woman can't see how important the almighty dollar is to him. And he wonders if she'll ever know what a dollar is really worth, what it really costs him to pursue it, and she wonders if he'll ever know how much it means to her to allow him into her body.

Men's bodies, as much as our parents' influences and our culture's shaping, makes us into the men we are. The way men view their bodies as machines they own to get their heads from place to place explains why men are so prone to point to things outside themselves and declare them, too, to be their property. Other people, money, prestige, power become potent fuel to a man's mechanical body. He turns these things into energy to keep him working seventy hours a week so he can buy more things to keep him going. His body hurts, but he can't rest, because he thinks he'll fall behind or he'll hear a voice inside his head telling him how lazy he is. He can't nurture his body because he doesn't know how. His father showed him how to shut it down with alcohol or TV, should the pain and the longing for love and touch become unbearable.

The very physiology of a man's body points to heavy labor. His shoulders can carry a world; his back, the burden of everyone who depends on him, and some who don't. But his chest is often collapsed and caved in by the fear of what he would feel if it were open.

A woman's body brings in the world to her. Women take men inside their own bodies and hold their love and their seed for days, weeks, or months. Some choose to hold inside them a new life for what seems like an eternity. Their breasts beckon the infant to them, and while their backs and shoulders are strong, and often carry as many pounds of pressure and pain as any man, they still don't quite under-stand what all men's external referencing is about.

Our fathers traded their bodies for money to show they were men. Our mothers traded their bodies for security and protection. They "took care" of our dads, and our dads "took care" of our moms. I almost never saw my dad treat my mom as an equal. I almost never saw my mom treat my dad that way either. Either Dad treated her like a daughter or a mother, or Mom treated him like a son or her dad. He pointed his body toward hers, she toward his, and yet some-how for me, there was No-Body at home.

Men are beginning to believe that they are some-body and that, while they can't be everything to every-body, they can be more open and more honest with themselves and the ones they love.

# THE WOUNDED LOVER

## The Walls Between Men and the Women They Love

He's there, behind the walls he's carefully created. Women know he's there. Their vision penetrates his walls and allows them to see clear through to his soul.

The woman sees in the man such "potential." If she just loves him enough and really understands him, she thinks he'll tear down those walls and come out to meet her. Until then, her job, her duty (as her mother taught her) is to wait until he wakes up and emerges. Then he can give her all the things her parents forgot or couldn't give to her as a child. A man can become a woman's favorite "project."

A man might be very conscious of his walls on days when his lover is not her usual self, when she's just a bit more needy than he is. He wants to reach out and help her like he used to want to help his mom. He wants to fix her but he can't, so he writes her a check and tries to buy her happiness. He expresses his love like his father did when he couldn't simply say, "I love you."

When a woman gives up her life to help a man realize his potential, he does not love her for it. When a man lets a woman turn him into a project, he gives more of his dignity away than he feels good about. And when a man buys a woman's affections with something other than his presence and love, she resents him for it. If you listen closely you can hear them silently scream the words "I hate you. I love you. Good-bye."

If the man doesn't run first—to another city, another lover or to solitude—the woman will usually leave. For she cannot be a widow to a potential lover who is buried in denial, hiding both from her and the unhealed wounds of his childhood.

When the woman goes, the man's walls shake, bricks fall out, and a space is created that leaves his heart and guts unprotected. Everything that ever hurt him, everybody who ever left him stands before him to be dealt with—to be felt— to be grieved. When a man is wounded, most healthy women won't be attracted to him.

While a wounded man may be on his way to wholeness, he's not ready to take another companion. Women who don't need or want to fix a man stay away and secretly hope that he'll get worse, then better. Women who are healthy are simply someplace else, and they say prayers for the dying man, hoping he has the strength and patience to heal himself.

A man must take down the walls that were built after each consecutive wound from childhood through adulthood by himself. He can be loved and supported in the process, but a woman who loves a walled-up man has her own work to do. She will heal only when she lets him go and cares enough about herself to battle her own demonic memories of father, mother, and all the men she meant to heal but only crippled further, damaging herself in the process.

Each man must in turn face the darkness and the face of each woman he held hostage with his pain, his intensity, and his own potential to heal, of which he may also be afraid.


## WHERE WALLS ARE BUILT, NO BOUNDARIES EXIST

He walks into the mountains of the Santa Fe National Forest and knows exactly who he is. He pulls in a sail as he glides into Pensacola's beautiful white bay and knows what he believes. He comes in from a business trip and slaps his briefcase on the dining-room table and knows where he lives.

Put a woman, a lover, in his life, and his shoulders and eyes, if not his lips, tell you he's lost. After each woman leaves or is driven off, he always draws to himself another lover, and loses himself again shortly after.

For years women have known about "giving up their power" or "losing themselves in their man" or "becoming what he wants them to be." Women have spoken about this problem in women's groups, in books, and to each other in friendly conversation. They've described how very often after a woman gets free from a relationship, she starts therapy or joins a support group and begins looking at her past, her pain, and her patterns. She often contacts old friends whom she had forgotten. She might return to school, or go after that executive position she gave up right after they were married. In any case, after a few months, she begins to get strong and clear, and she radiates the message, "I'm fine, I'm powerful, I'm happy, and I don't need a man to make me whole."

Bingo—a man sees her and is attracted. Three months later, she's lost her power, and her personality has meshed into his. She says silently to herself, "Hell, I didn't know what to do with all that health, energy, and power anyway. Just like my mamma taught me, I need a man to help me, to make me truly whole."

Lots of women have admitted to falling into this harmful pattern. It's time that men admit to it as well. For we men lose ourselves, too. We often give up who we are, even in the company of women we don't know, let alone with the one we love. If we enter a room that contains female strangers, we change and say things and do things we wouldn't normally do.

A man by himself may begin to think he's healed. He bets Buddhahood is not that far out of reach, water might just be walked on, and codependency is just a label he used to wear reluctantly. Six weeks into an intimate relationship and he's aware that he's closer to Bubba-hood, he feels like he's drowning, and he probably needs to go back into therapy and attend a Twelve-Step group as well.

When I'm alone, I get up every morning, have a cup of tea, take a short walk, do some yoga, eat a good breakfast at a decent hour, read the paper, and then write for forty-five minutes to an hour. Until . . . I get with a woman. Then it went something like this: 10:00 A.M., still in bed. I don't have to walk today. Yeah, I know it's been several days since I wrote. . . . And so it goes. On top of that, I would stop calling and seeing my friends and doing many of the things I loved. In other words, I'd lose my routine, my sanity-making rituals, my discipline—my self. Not that rituals, routines, and disciplines are who I am, but they help me stay in touch with my inner being and my higher power, and they help keep me peaceful and productive.

I'm not saying that rituals and discipline shouldn't give way to other priorities from time to time. What I am saying is that men often give up parts of themselves entirely in order to please their partners, and most don't even know when they're doing so until much later—sometimes too late. This unconscious "giving up" lowers men's self-esteem and self-worth. In the end, men often resent and blame women, as if women asked men to give themselves up.

Only recently have I realized that it was my whole self that my lover was attracted to in the first place, just as I was attracted to that powerful woman who became so strong and healthy after the divorce or separation. When I gave up my power, she may even have felt cheated, as if she were with another man, a lesser version of whom she fell in love with.

When I was by myself I'd stay close to myself; things from the outside came in. I'd see the sunsets, I'd hear the birds, I'd watch the clouds, and feel the wind blow across my face. I beheld the many faces of God, and creation gave me energy and sustained me. When I'd get with a woman, my energy would shoot out to her and she, through no intent of her own, would come between me and those things I just mentioned, and most importantly, between me and myself.

When we'd break up, I'd take walks, and the world would become alive again. And I'd always be sad that in my disease of codependency, I could not sustain contact with myself while in the relationship. I used to have to leave in order to reconnect with what I valued and what I needed.

I have finally started learning how to simply and truly be—and how to be simply, truly with a partner and continue to be who I am when I'm with her. It's getting easier and easier with time.

## THE ROMANCE IS NOT THE JOURNEY

This losing of ourselves—the selves we've never quite found—in relationships, is one of the things that makes men so reluctant to commit. At the first part of a relationship many men still feel free, unattached, like an anchorless ship ready to make a journey. We look at ourselves in the mirror and see a face of a hunter who searches for the "one" who will make us "whole," the one who will give meaning and purpose to our life. Even though we really know better than to believe that one person can solve our problems, we just don't know how to fill the hole we carry deep inside ourselves where a solid sense of self should be.

The voyage into a relationship excites and enlivens us. Most men know that traveling somewhere is better and more fun than arriving there. Remember those trips we used to take across the country that sometimes lasted longer than our stay at the final destination? The going was great, but if we stayed there for too long we turned into a resistant resident who must settle down and become a householder or a businessman, a farmer, a friend, or perhaps a husband.

For many men wandering around looking for romance, the wine, the elegant dinners, the conversation, and sex that lasted until dawn temporarily filled us and fed our hungry hearts. Romance, and the drama and intensity that come along with it, numb while simultaneously intoxicating us, all the while making us forget that our lover cannot fill the empty spaces. But in the early stages of a romance, we forget most of what we know and nearly all that we learned from the last lover.

When the romantic music stops and the conversation turns to family, finance, or frequency of sex, the wounded man leaves. He does not leave physically, at least not at first, but he begins to leave in more subtle ways—he doesn't listen or he escapes into fantasy, TV, alcohol, or work. He leaves because his true journey is his search for his own "deep masculinity," although at the time most do not know this is the case. But something deep inside him knows that his quest for himself has been preempted and sidetracked.

If a man drives off his lover or leaves her, he feels free again to pursue that which has eluded him for so long. Paradoxically, as soon as she's gone and he feels safe, he also feels soulless and confused. At that moment he may even ask the very woman he just pushed away to come back. If she does, he feels satisfied for a time, but then once again begins backing off in preparation for the next leg of his journey toward his own soul. But before he finds his own wandering soul he's once again looking for his soul's mate.

A lot of women will try to be soul mates to men without souls. These women are then confused and angry when they are treated like replacement parts for a man's failing heart. Men tend to leave or run women off who want commitments and want to make a journey toward wholeness together, but women still choose men who prefer the chase to the destination of intimacy.

Women also choose men with fictitious personalities. In

Woody Allen's *The Purple Rose of Cairo*, Cecilia is married to a wounded man. One of the ways she deals with her loneliness and lack of intimacy is to fill as many of her vacant moments as possible by going to the movies. She especially loves the romantic ones where the boy gets the girl and the girl seems to get all the love women everywhere want. On one lonely afternoon, while her husband is out with the boys gambling, the Saturday afternoon matinee's romantic lead steps off the screen and into the very theater where she sits. She falls in love and says, "He's the kind of man a girl always dreams about. He's fictional. But then nothing's perfect."

Men have been living fictional lives for a long time. Some try to be Gatsbys, others try to mimic a Hemingway hero. Others try to be cool, unaffected, and unemotional like many of the characters Clint Eastwood plays. Fiction gives us many role models for our masculinity. Women buy our fictitious personalities like dime-store novels. Our covers look great and have lots of sex appeal, but our contents lack in substance.

And yet women keep buying the lines and the stories and wondering why they keep having the same unfortunate, predictable endings. They really want to believe that the next character they love will be real.

Most men don't even know they are living "make-believe" lives until about the second act—during the divorce or the breakup. Then they discover, and some regret, that their characters are not fully developed. They wish they could rewrite the scenes that left many hearts broken, but they don't know how.

But many men *are* trying to become "real," to separate fantasy from fact, separate themselves from their fathers and mothers, and separate truth from fiction. They are trying to show up for a relationship rather than merely put on a good show for three or four months.

Women need to stop wanting cardboard heroes, to face their own woundedness and demand that their lovers be real with them and feel with them and give and receive nurturing, while ever increasing their capacity for intimacy and joy. And a woman who has really worked on herself will slowly begin not to accept less than a good solid "human" effort by her partner. If women still want wounded men to take care of and mother back to health, they will find themselves attracted to men who will not know they have holes in their chest where their hearts should be, who refuse even to try to learn the difference between a feeling and a hammer. Like Cecilia these women will have to settle for a silver screen lover and live with their needs unmet.

While a woman should not have to wait on anyone to take responsibility for his own pain, she must be patient with the ones who do. She needs to know we are slow to heal, even slower to feel, and we're a little hesitant and unsure of this new masculinity, and how women will respond to it. We'll be awkward at first with this new freedom to be ourselves and be loved for who we are, not what we do or become. It's hard to share from a place inside us that has been sealed off for a long time. If a man is trying, stay with him, support him, but don't try to do it for him or he'll have to leave because that will be mothering him and every man must leave a mother in order to grow up. He can, at times, do what he must do and feel with you, and at other times he'll have to do it alone or in the company of men. You may also want to know that we'll want to rush our recovery and most of us are not very patient with ourselves or anyone else for that matter. We'll want to make up for all the past mistakes. We'll need to take the time to learn to ask for what we need. But we will, as soon as we feel safe enough to do so and have some practice at it. We're willing to try.

The fear wounded men have of deep involvement and intimacy is linked to the fear of being pressured and smothered, abandoned or absorbed. If a man can learn to separate his early fears and longings from the vulnerabilities he feels in a relationship, he can learn to heal while being in love. But if, while he's in a relationship, he keeps a back door open or keeps his eye on the front door to see who else might walk in, he will never have to face his fears.

One reason men are afraid to give up the hunt and make a commitment is that they fear they may become like their fathers—haunted, stalked, and scared by their wives, parents, or bosses. A man "who remains inside his own house, stays there, inside the dishes and in the glasses . . ." (Rilke). When a son does not face his fears about his manliness, his disappointments about his father, his father's inadequacy, he runs the risk of becoming lifeless and angry and empty. He risks turning from his emptiness to drown his fears in alcohol, gambling, to silence the ache in his gut, or to drugging himself with work and coke to make himself forget that he didn't do the soul work that his father also should have done. Recognizing and releasing the fathers in us can break down the walls between the inner parts of ourselves, our lovers, and between other men.


## WALLS, WARS, COWBOYS, AND WARRIORS

As boys, we grew up in the suburbs or the city or on farms, waging make-believe wars in the jungles of the Philippines and on Pork Chop Hill in Korea. We turned sticks into Thompson submachine guns, rocks into grenades, and ourselves into someday soldiers.

We rode on stallions through the deserts of Arizona and fought at the Alamo alongside Davy Crockett and Jim Bowie. We died only on the days we weren't the "good guy." On those awful afternoons in the backyard or the park when the luck of the draw turned us into a "Jap," a "Commie," an "Injun," or a "Mexican," we could still be thankful we weren't a "Nazi."

When it rained, war was waged indoors. Toy soldiers and calvary and Indians were pitted against each other. The thrills of victory or the agonizing cries of defeat were muffled so as not to disturb the sleeping civilians while we made the country a safe place for women, children, and democracy. When there were no comrades-in-arms to play with due to a cold or our failure to take out the garbage, we'd turn on the tube and let Audie Murphy or John Wayne do the fighting for us.

Since the day we were born, society has psychologically prepared us to go to war, to kill or be killed. We've been taught to hold in anger or rage until that moment when it can be unleashed on another race, in a country other than our own.

Do you know how much anger has to be in a boy before he can kill another man, a woman, or a child? How much fear must be bred into a man who goes into an alien jungle and then decides who lives and who dies? Do you understand how armored a boy must be to play games that include strangulation, decapitation, maiming, and cursing people of other colors for being on the same planet as himself?

Most boys go numb long before they are attracted to

women. They grow up in a culture that glorifies the warrior archetype way beyond what is healthy. War may be necessary at times, but a warrior unable to weep and grieve the destruction he causes to himself and others should not be a model for young boys.

But we were ready to fight, most of us. We had been hardened and walled-off long before boot camp became a possibility. And if we did go to boot camp, most likely just as we were on the brink of manhood, we learned to hate our "enemy." If we didn't, we hated our drill sergeant so much we had to take our anger out on the enemy just to get basic training out of our systems.

A lover rides up to us just as we head for the sunset after doing a day's battle with "redskins" or "outlaws," and says, "Wait, I want to be with you. I want you to settle down or at least, let me ride into that sunset with you. You don't have to go it alone." And we say, "Shucks, ma'am, I'd like to stay, but there's a wilderness to be tamed, Injuns to be fought, bad men to be put behind bars. Maybe I'll be back this way someday." With a tip of the hat, the music swells up and the hero rides off unable to feel a thing.

Women wonder why we men can't open up, let them in, share our feelings, and theirs. It's because we're still looking for the war on the outside that we were prepared and programmed to fight, and we can't find it. With armor intact and submachines, grenades, and pistols packed in our briefcases and our psyches, we wage the war in corporate clashes, in football stadiums, or in keeping up with the Joneses.

But mostly we wage it inside ourselves where plastic soldiers never sleep, John Wayne never dies, and Geronimo is still on the loose. There women and children are meant to be protected, not to have feelings about; and there anger builds until we fight, or until it bursts arteries and hearts and marriages.

When the man who grew up prepared to kill, programmed for war, holds a baby or a woman in his arms, if he holds one at all, he will look at him or her and feel very, very far away.

## WALLS OF NICENESS

They smile a lot. They take all the responsibility for everything. They try real hard to guess what you need: they almost never say "no." They are called "Nice Guys." They're gentlemen who very often live in "nice" homes, drive "nice" cars, have "nice" children and "nice" wives. Most of them were raised by "nice parents" who taught them to be nice no matter what. These nice men believe that all the dysfunctional patterns they have in their lives were created by themselves without any help from anyone else.

These men are very often afraid to look closely at their families and early experiences. And when I ask them how they became unable to express feelings, they usually say, "I don't know. I guess I've always been that way."

"You didn't know how to express sadness and anger as a baby?" I ask.

"Well, of course I could as a baby. All babies can cry and scream and get angry, but then one day I couldn't. I just went numb."

And right after that, they went Nice. They laugh even when they're angry and later they figure out subtle ways to get even. They say "yes" when what they really mean is, "hell, no." They go places they don't want to go and look as if they like it. They make teachers, preachers, grandparents, uncles and aunts, and most of all parents very proud. They get praised for being nice; and they rarely get talked about or put down. To them it seems like everybody is either "nice" or nasty. They never learned that somewhere in between nice and no-good lies a middle ground to be stood upon firmly where positions are to be taken, boundaries drawn, and places created where no one can trespass. Somehow they were taught that only an asshole would say no to a lover or wife. Only assholes get angry and draw lines, ask for what they need and tell people what they feel. Only callous men say, "Enough," "Stop," "No more."

People who don't need to be nice say all these things when it's appropriate. They also look at their family history and see that someone—a father, mother, uncle, or big brother—taught them how to stuff their feelings. Then they feel the anger and grief about their childhood and they begin to heal rather than denying or blaming themselves for what they were shown.

"Nice guys" do finish last, because no one really wants to be around them for very long. They eventually create their worst fantasy, they're left, abandoned, ignored, unloved. Real intimacy is banished in the Kingdom of Nice.

Women have told me dozens of times how "nice" their husbands or lovers are, but how they can't get angry. These men can't stand to see others angry either. Very often they let their lovers walk all over them because they're afraid their lovers will leave them. They try to fix their mates or their relationships rather than feeling and encouraging their loved ones to feel. They hope the other will be as nice as they try to be.

66

These same nice men turn into the men who often finally pull a driver out of his car and beat the crap out of him for not yielding or putting on his turn signal. These same nice guys, who have stuffed their rage so long in peacetime, in wartime unleash their rage on other soldiers and innocents.

I was brought up to be one of these nice men. I never yelled or made an ugly face or told anyone how I was really feeling inside. The truth is I was angry, hurt, lonely, afraid, and full of wonder, and I hid all those parts of me.

And I did it so people would think I was nice, that I came from a nice family who went to a nice church and lived in a nice house. Until I stopped trying to "be nice" I couldn't learn how to stop being passive-aggressive, verbally abusive, cold, indifferent, and prejudiced.

Now I know people love me because I'm a man capable of genuinely being nice when I feel nice inside and being angry and scared and able to state my truth when it's called for. I'm not "nice." I'm a man—a human being who can be nice and can be uncaring and cold, but is usually simply somewhere in-between.

The real war that is to be fought is within our souls. To win the war for ourselves, we will have to stop being nice and take some time away from romance and perhaps wander around in the woods with other men who are willing to fight their dads and their demons and take back their energy, their power, and heal their wounded masculinity.

# PART TWO

# THE JOURNEY

# A GATHERING IN THE WOODS

## Uncovering the Wound

"The woods are lovely, dark and deep.
But I have promises to keep,
And miles to go before I sleep."

Robert Frost

I t's been cloudy and raining in Austin for more than thirty days now. Men are arriving at the Men's Center from all over the country to gather and travel to the woods where they will sleep on the ground, gaze at the stars, and uncover their wounds and grieve for them under the foreboding skies and moon-hidden nights. Men come alone or in small groups of twos and threes from Michigan, Georgia, New Mexico, California, Florida, and Ohio. One is even from my old home state of Alabama, although he now lives in California.

The men who pile out, leap out, or reluctantly drag themselves out are as varied as the machines that bring them. Tony, a banker from New York, looks as if he stopped at Banana Republic before heading to Texas. Richard wears a beard that would have made any ex-hippie envious, though he never smoked a joint in his life. Roger is in his late fifties and yet wouldn't look a day over thirty-five were it not for all the gray in his hair. He makes his living as an account executive for a large advertising firm in Dallas. And Bob wears unusual, colorful clothes that he designed himself and sells at arts and crafts fairs all over the country. Even though the men come from all walks of life, they find many men here with similar backgrounds, interests, eccentricities, and wounds.

Energy and enthusiasm pervade the Men's Center despite the weather. Yet I can also sense the pain and emptiness so many of the men carry with them. I'm sure a good number of them hope to leave behind their feelings of isolation in the woods, to beat their anger out on the drums we'll take with us, and somehow come to understand the roles and patterns that have kept them from feeling whole for so long. While it's unlikely that they'll accomplish this in one weekend, many of them may come close to doing all three.

What I notice most about the men who attend men's gatherings or support groups is a remarkable and paradoxical combination of fear and courage. I can see it in the men who walk in today. Their fear comes from having never been able to trust other men. As I've pointed out already, if you grow up with an untrustworthy father who can't be there for you, who abuses you through neglect, criticism, shame, whippings, beatings, or lies, it becomes hard to trust men you've known your whole life, much less a group of more than a hundred men you've never met. Of the one hundred and thirty men attending this weekend, nearly all will have a wound from their father, one they have likely hidden from themselves for years, although men with sensitive eyes and ears could detect it after only a few minutes in their presence.

Many of them also have a general fear of the unknown, of what will come up in their emotions, from their memories, and their pasts. For most, it's their first time at a men's gathering. Nevertheless, we men who grew up in unhealthy, rigid, controlling families need to look like we've done everything before, like we always know what we're doing. Most men grew up believing that it was a crime, a sin, not to be always in charge and in control. We were taught by our fathers that it was weakness to "not know." When we get lost or confused while traveling, we'd rather die than admit it. There was a time when I would drive for hours before I'd pull into a gas station and ask for directions. I needed to pretend to know where I was even though I'd never been there before. We have mastered the look, the stance, that will make it seem that we always know what we're doing.

Men have been told for a lifetime that they are sick at best, scum at worst. I heard a joke that someone was writing a new book called *The Goddess in Every Woman: The Scum in Every Man*. After all, didn't we learn as children that girls are made from "sugar and spice and everything nice" and boys are made from crawly insects and animal anuses—snails and puppy dog tails. Many men grow up thinking that being a man is a nasty thing, that men are less than human.

Some mothers subtly undermined our self-esteem as men by saying such things as, "Men. You can't trust any of them," or, "Men are no good." Others saw their mothers verbally abuse their dads. The culture as a whole, while sexist and patriarchal, still blames men for the waste, the wars, and the repercussion of wars. Even today, television depicts men as stumbling boobs who can't tie their own shoelaces.

Many men watched their fathers do so many horrible things, say undermining things about other men, attack small countries, pets, and children, that they knew firsthand that adult men were brutal, uncaring, and insensitive.

The men who attend groups and gatherings have chosen not to live with such images any longer. They want to find a new image of masculinity and a new meaning for the word "man." They are ready to shed their old skins. They arrive at the gatherings thinking their sickness of mind, body, and spirit forces them to face their demons. But really their courage has led them there. The truly "sick" men are still not identifying their problems and will not come to men's groups, men's centers, men's gatherings, or read books about men's wounds. Those men are still very likely projecting their problems onto women, children, other men, and other nations. The men who come to heal are by and large the healthiest men on the planet. They realize they need help and healing. They are strong enough to admit they hurt, and to say, "I'm scared, but I'm here. I will show up and face my pain." And after a few hours in the company of other supportive men, many will reveal their fears for what is for some, the first time in their lives.

As the carsful of men drive up to the Bosque Creek Ranch, two and a half hours away from Austin, the sun shows itself for the first time in weeks. The weekend has begun.

## RECLAIMING THE BODY

The first night, men gather around the fire and lean in closer when someone speaks about how he couldn't love the women he wanted to, the women who loved him. Tom says in a half-broken voice, "I don't know why I'm here, except that my life just isn't working. I'm treating my kids like Dad treated me and I'm working on my second divorce." Frank steps into the firelight and looks at the men's faces. "I've got to connect with you guys. I've got to know I ain't crazy for wanting men friends to share all this pain I've been carrying with me for thirty years." Burt stands up. "My dad's going to go into an old folks' home next month. If I don't do this work, he's going to die without knowing how I really feel. Hell, I'm going to die without knowing." Miguel stands and says, "My wife said I should come." Fred laughs and says, "My therapist said I should."

After working with hundreds of men and receiving hundreds of letters from men who have read my books, *The Flying Boy* and *I Don't Want to Be Alone*, I have realized that these men do want to love, but that they cannot or do not know how to love. When a woman asks to be let in to their hearts, they cannot find the door. Many men look very hard for the door, many more get frustrated and quit looking, and others go to work and try to earn a paycheck they can turn over and just call it love. Some men just crawl inside a bottle or a bag of dope and die from the pain of not being able to express their feelings to her or themselves.

It isn't that we don't want and need love as much as women do, or that we deliberately set out to reject, or not feel the love that is freely given. We cannot receive the love that women special-deliver because we aren't at home in our bodies.

You see, some men are finally beginning to see and feel the fact that the only way they love is if there is somebody at home to get the gift. It takes most men many sessions of individual or group counseling and lots of support before they begin to get to the feelings that reside in the body. Most men do not know or remember that they have a body. They grew up in their heads, having turned away from their bodies, their wounds, their grief. Sadness, grief, longing, joy, anger, and disappointment are not simply intellectual constructs, but genuine feelings created in the stomach, back, and chest. If men can't feel their bodies because they are numb, and they keep numbing them with all sorts of addictions, their wounds stay buried inside the bones and tissues that were ignored, beaten, or buried when they were boys. The grief that lives in each shoulder, stomach, jaw, back, buttock, leg, arm, hand, and heart cannot be released. Without bringing their bodies into the recovery process, they remain "talking heads" aiming toward self-destruction.

For instance, when I ask a man how he feels about his father, he often pauses for a long time. Nine out of ten, he'll cock his head to the side and look upward, and answer, "I think my father did the best he could. He worked hard and provided well for us . . ." And so it goes.

"But how do you *feel* about your father," I repeat.

"I just told you," they say, impatiently.

Gently, I remind them that they told me what they *thought* not what they *felt*.

Reclaiming the body is one of the main goals of the men's movement. It is the only way we can fully move into our wounds and out into the world less wounded than we began. Many men—and women—may not understand how to get their bodies back. Some ways to experience the body are through movement—dance, drumming, pushing, pulling, beating a pillow, pounding the earth with a tree limb; and sound—screaming, crying, shouting, speaking out, singing.

While many men have screamed or pushed or even beaten drums, they've done so without focusing on their rage, anger, grief, and guilt. Without consciously using these movements to rid the body of repressed emotions, the movements do little to heal. For instance, a man can play racketball for fun or he can play to release his anger. If he's angry, but afraid to feel it, the racketball game is merely exercise and competition. If he is telling himself and his partner that he is full of feelings that need to come out, however, every movement can become cathartic and cleansing.

By taking our armor off in the presence of other men, we move toward regaining our lost ability to be intimate. Intimacy, as I define it, is the ability to share feelings when they come up in an appropriate way, without wounding through guilt or criticism. It is also listening to others share their feelings, too. Without being in touch with our bodies, we can't feel our feelings or other people's, nor can we share our feelings or hear others'. We can't let love in.

If we're alienated from our own bodies we stop breathing when others are expressing their feelings, and our bodies signal to theirs, saying, "Stop, I'm not comfortable enough in my own body to allow you to continue." And if we've lived with the belief that shame or sadness is "all in our heads," then we try to convince others that's where their pain is. We tell people in distress that if they'll only "understand" they'll be all right. Most men who come to gatherings and men's groups wish *understanding* was all they needed, but they *feel* a need for more.

My dad used to say to me, "I don't see why you can't figure out what's wrong and fix it. You're smart and well-educated. You'd *think* by now you'd *understand* what's going wrong in your relationships and stop doing what you've been doing. You've read all those books. Don't they explain everything?"

I know women have been wrongly taught by our culture to use their bodies as seductive tools—but at least most have been taught that they had bodies. When I tell a roomful of men that part of their journey will consist in "getting their bodies back," they may look at me as if to say, "What the hell is this guy talking about? My body brought me here, didn't it?" Most men I've met believe their bodies have a duty to perform even though it screams for attention now and then with ulcers, backaches, and fatigue. We have learned dozens of legal ways to deny the pain that exists in our bodies. And the pain becomes so pronounced after years of betraying, denying, and abusing the body that most men are afraid to feel it.

"You can do anything you put your mind to," my dad said over and over again. I listened and believed that if I really wanted to drive the twenty-four hours it takes to go from Boulder to Birmingham I could do it. And I did. But at a high cost to my body. The way I did it was by stuffing caffeine, nicotine, and alcohol into that twenty-five-year-old body, already buzzed on adrenaline and my father's words, "mind over matter." My back, legs, and butt begged my brain for a room in a Motel 6. My head would say "shut up" to my body's complaints and aches. "We can do it, besides, we can't afford a motel anyway. I'll get more coffee at the next truck stop."

Some men use up their bodies in professional sports by the time they're thirty. An amateur wrestler once told me of his many surgeries, the pins placed, and the pain that came before the age of twenty-five. Another man told me how he worked out for hours a day and damn near starved himself to death to remain attractive to women at forty-five when nature was broadening and balding him in spite of his efforts and ego.

And then there's war. Men must detach from their bodies in order to fight a war, see a war waged on CNN, or report a war on CNN. Once, during an interview with Bernard Shaw, I heard the plight of the American male who must fight in any war. When Shaw returned from his assignment in Baghdad, after those first numbing days of the war that he witnessed from his hotel room, he was asked how he could keep reporting (he did so by leaning out his window and going up on the roof). The answer made feel me so sad. He said he did so by not allowing himself "to feel" in order to "objectively report" and "do his job." The point he was making was that if he had "felt anything" he couldn't have continued. If men could feel they couldn't continue a lot of what they do, see done, know is being done, not only to *their* bodies but the bodies of their brothers, sisters, and children, those whom they know, and those they have never met.

We shut our bodies down, find the switch inside our heads that reads "off," and flip it. It stays frozen in that position for years. It starts when we're small. As a boy I was never taught that my body was sensual and important. I remember, after doing much body-oriented therapy

(Bioenergetics and Rolfing), sitting in a bathtub one day, something I rarely did because showers are quicker. I just soaked. I took handfuls of delightful peppermint soap and gently stroked my legs and arms just like I cared for them because they were a part of me, just like it was okay to touch my own body and enjoy the sensuality of it all, however strange and foreign the feeling was. I realized that I had lived over three decades and never really slowly, lovingly bathed my own body. I take lots of baths now and no longer wonder why so many of the women I've known and know bathe in candlelight and take an hour to do so.

If we can learn to get in touch with and honor our own bodies, we will be well on the way to finding a part of ourselves that has been hidden—our true selves—our deep masculinity. We will put our bodies and souls back together again. By placing ourselves in a men's group, our bodies will shake with fear as our souls delight in the opportunity they have been waiting for, for decades.

## PUTTING BODY AND SOUL TOGETHER AGAIN

The men's group provides a safer place to realize and feel how the body retains memories like an emotional sponge and that men must wring it out regularly if the body is to keep working in an efficient, functional, and loving way. The body is a charge-building system and if it is not discharged on a regular basis, then we develop disease and addictions that keep us from remembering ourselves, from recognizing our original hurts and wounds. Disease sidetracks us by making us focus on the disease's cure rather than its cause; addictions numb the awareness of the original core wound. If I drink, eat, or screw enough, I can forget I have a body.

By forgetting the body, men also forget their souls. Many of the men I've worked with have a strong connection to their spirits, but their souls are full of holes and almost totally neglected as their fathers' souls were.

The soul is in the body. When we find our bodies, we heal our souls. The spirit is more ethereal, more elevated; it may even reside in our heads. The soul likes drums and the body likes to beat drums. The spirit is moved by more melodic sounds. The soul likes dancing and pounding on a pillow, or the earth—it is primitive. The spirit likes prayer and meditation.

Many men, even athletes, have lost their bodies. When some men exercise or do yoga or Tai Chi, they do it with their heads. Watch their faces. Often their energy will be concentrated in their heads and eyes. The expression is one of tension, striving—the mind over matter kind of look.

Tony is a martial arts expert. His body is perfect by GQ standards. His black belt is wrapped around a thirty-two-inch waist, and his shoulders are square and level. He works out five or six days a week and looks as if he knows his body and loves it. At a workshop, I asked Tony to tell me how it felt to lose his father in Vietnam. He stared off in the distance and said, "I don't really feel anything." His body was built by Nautilus equipment. His energy and grace of movement was made in the Orient. But his pain, his grief, and his anger were on Mars. He was as far away from his body when it came to remembering, feeling, and expressing feelings as any man I've worked with.

We've not only been taught not to feel our bodies, we've been taught to avoid at all cost the feeling of emptiness that exists right after we've really discharged our emotions, if we ever happen to do so. After a good cry or release of anger, I'll ask a man how he feels. Very often, after saying "better" or "lighter" or "good," he'll say "empty."

Our parents taught us by example never to be caught feeling "empty." Put something in—food, drink, work, sex, something, but don't ever feel empty. And yet, the body's unspoken, unconscious goal is to be empty as much as possible. It provides us with natural release mechanisms, like crying, by which we can empty ourselves out. Once done, that space most men feel in their stomachs, chests, hearts, and backs can then be filled with foreign feelings like joy and happiness, which also must be felt, experienced, expressed—emptied out to make room for the next wave of feelings about to wash up. The soul and the body, the mind and the spirit, must be united, and the emptier we become, the more room we have to let those who love us share that room.

Some people may need a body-oriented therapy to help them remember their bodies. Therapies like Bioenergetics, Rolfing, Hakaomi, Neo-Reichien, Feldenkrais, as well as others that bring us down into our bodies, may be very useful in certain stages of one's recovery. These forms of body-work release the pain and the memories out of frozen, stiff, armored bone, muscles, tissues, and organs. Sometimes they can help us recall the things that we needed for a time to forget, but that we are now ready to deal with and heal because we have the support to do so.

It's important to remember that our bodies and our emotions need to be worked with regularly. Our weekend of discharging emotion at a men's group is not enough to reconnect the body and soul. This reconnection needs to happen consciously, and often. At first, you might find yourself slipping back into your early mode of suppressing your emotions and repressing your body, of being only a "nice" guy. Try to stay committed to honoring your feelings, your joy, as well as your anger. If your boss or wife says something, or does something you have strong feelings about, feel those feelings, experience them, and share them with someone rather than numbing them out with drugs, work, or TV. Keeping your body and emotions connected means making an active, willful effort week after week until reconnecting becomes an automatic process—which it will. And it will give you more energy, more happiness, than ignoring and burying your feelings and your body.

## FEELING OUR ANGER

When the journey takes a man into his body and through his losses at points and places along the way, he'll confront the fact that if his father had been there for him as a boy, adolescent, and young man, the bumps, bruises, and abuse he'd received and perpetuated would have been fewer and farther between. When a man feels the fact that his father was absent, he then feels anger and grief.

Expressing this anger and grief takes wildly different forms. One man at this men's gathering screamed and made the hairs of those who were within earshot bristle. Another man took a red plastic bat and beat a pillow, shouting, "I hate you, you son-of-a-bitch" two dozen times, and finished the last blow by saying, "because I loved you so much." Still another man sat in the middle of a circle of a dozen men and wept for many minutes that represented a childhood, a lifetime.

Of all the ways I know to get our bodies back, become intimate, and let people in, the process of grieving is most effective. Men who can grieve, men who can wail in the night, will be able to dance at dawn. If they can learn to feel their pain, they will stop projecting it onto others, and they can feel others' pain without becoming responsible for it or having to fix it. The door to the body, the passageway to intimacy is through grief.

Men who come to the men's gatherings, to men's groups, and to Twelve-Step recovery programs, come in large part to grieve; they come to get their bodies back. And when men have gone to many meetings or gatherings, they will be different—stronger, steadier, and gentler, but *not* softer. They will have seen for themselves men nurturing other men without a woman anywhere around. They will have seen that the ability to nurture is in themselves and always has been. They will be better able to comfort their children with supportive arms and less shaming tones in their voices. They will make love more and be "fucking angry" a lot less. They will know the benefit of tears and they will have started to let go of ghost fathers and mothers. They will hope that those who stayed home can begin to do the same.

Men who say they don't need to do these things are fewer in number than they used to be. Moving into a deeper masculinity cannot be done without grieving the loss of the father. I wish I could say that all the anger and the sadness comes out in one gathering, one two-hour men's group. It doesn't. Allowing himself to feel grief and anger whenever it arises makes a man a man. Denying his feelings keeps him a boy and keeps the women he loves at bay.

84

The healing process is beginning for the men at this gathering; they have a lot more work to do, but they are now willing, committed. The men who screamed and cried in rage and grief at their fathers' betrayals have shed a tear and glimpsed the child inside themselves. They have reconnected their bodies and souls and felt the emptiness of discharging their woundedness. Through this a man has been born. The journey is underway.

## THE JOURNEY'S BAPTISM: STARTING OVER

On the first morning of the gathering, the sky opened and the rain descended on us once again. My coleader Marvin Allen and I discussed what we should do as we'd accidentally left behind the large revival tent, and the other tents were too small to accommodate so many men at once. "Maybe we should just get naked and make this a real wildman weekend," I said jokingly. (Wildman is a term Robert Bly coined to describe that part of the male psyche and soul that is still spontaneous, earthy, primal, and vital.)

Instead we stood shuddering in our rain gear that was already getting soaked through. I struggled through my talk on the archetype of the "Mother," and the feminine side of men's psyches, but I knew something wasn't right. My heart wasn't in it, as the pounding rain seemed to make my words irrelevant.

By 9:00 A.M. the rain had let up. We wandered up to the sacred grove where we usually drum, dance, and storytell. Most of us moved halfheartedly. As we passed the parked cars, several men began contemplating getting back into their Fords and Toyotas and going back to their dry homes, and a few did.

Standing there half-soaked, it finally came to me: Take off your clothes. Stop lecturing. Stop trying to be in control of the weather and enjoy the water, a symbol for the feminine in nearly every culture's mythology.

Men's gatherings usually do not include nudity. Occasionally on a hot summer-day some of us will strip down to our birthday suits and jump into a nearby pond. And on Saturday nights we go naked into the purification lodges or sweat lodges that are led by Native Americans we invite to help guide us through their powerful cleansing ceremony. But for the most part, we're all too modest or embarrassed to take our clothes off.

I got scared for a moment. What will these men think if I strip naked? How will they feel? Will my body scare off those who almost didn't come in the first place? Will they think I'm an aging exhibitionist? Or will they think what my father and most of his generation would think, that I was revealing my latent homosexuality? Perhaps they'd think I was an idealistic escapee from Woodstock.

But in spite of my doubts and self-consciousness, I knew I had to get naked. By the time my clothes were off, much to my surprise, two or three others had done the same. And then several other men joined in. I came out of my clothes like a four-year-old ready to play (YEAH!), and play we did. Cry we did. Talk we did. Drum we did. Sing we did. Some of us slid into two large mudholes, rubbing mud on ourselves and each other with total abandonment. About half of the men remained fully clothed and stood watching and laughing and wondering why they couldn't get naked and muddy, too.

A few of the clothed men talked as the rain began to fall

harder. "My mom always said, 'Don't get wet; you'll catch cold and get sick and it could turn into pneumonia.'" Other men heard their mothers say, "You'll get sick and have to miss school."

One man said, "I'm afraid for men to see my body. I'm afraid they'll look at my penis and see how small it is." Marvin added jokingly, "Yeah, and in the rain and cold mine always shrinks." Another man spoke for dozens when he said, "I'm afraid men will see me looking at their bodies and think I want more than just to look."

A thirty-year-old man named Phillip stood up on a bale of hay and said, "My dad's here with me at this thing, and I'm afraid to take my clothes off for fear of what he'll think or that he'll be embarrassed by my nakedness. But I don't want my seven-year-old son ever to be embarrassed or ashamed of his body like I am. I'm going to take these clothes off for me and my son." He then looked at his father and began to strip. Just after he said the word "son" a dozen other fathers came out of their clothes in an attempt to break the legacy of shame they did not want to pass on.

The men who remained clothed were not pressured. I only hoped this glimpse of spontaneity and exuberance, this celebration of life and nature, would encourage them to break through their shame someday in a manner more comfortable to them.

It was a warm day and the rain felt good on my skin. As we stood there surrounding our fire—man's first invention—the flames and the rain and the ground and we were ten million years old. At this timeless moment my body went into the earth and the rain into my soul and I could breathe easily and peacefully again.

And not surprisingly I found—as I sensed others did—more of the "feminine" while celebrating the first female, Mother Earth, than I ever could have with a lecture, or some contrived experiential exercise. And as we got closer to Gaia, many of us were able to let go of the fearful mothers in our heads.

The next morning the sun rose and the rest of the day was as intense as the day before had been. Most of the men awoke early and were gazing at the sky as if it were holy. The weekend was wild beyond imagination and yet safe and very sane.

I realized more fully that in order to find our feminine soul we must first find our masculinity, and we do both by separating from the world of women from time to time and being in the company of men—just standing naked or clothed, facing a fire, finding our feelings, letting the rain, the sun, and each other into places we didn't even know we had, healing wounds we always wished would just go away by themselves.

# THE SWORD AND THE SHIELD

## Discovering Our True Masculinity

Metaphors are archaic yet powerful images. When fully understood and used in proper balance, the sword and shield can offer deep insight into the meaning of true masculinity in both men and women.

Put simply, true masculinity is the knowledge and ability to know when to raise the sword, when to cut with it, and when to sheath it. True masculinity also knows when to hold the shield instead of a sword when confronted by a foe.

Raise the sword and say stop, don't hit that child again. Don't come across this line I draw in the sand, on the carpet, on my body, or in my soul. Do not call me names. Do not push me beyond my limits. Cease.

Cut when the relationship is dead. Cut the umbilical cord that is stretched from Florida to California. Sever the ties to friends who can't support your recovery. Cut the crap.

Sheath the sword in silence when an apology is heartfully

offered. Put the sword in its case when the partner commits in earnest to find help for his or her codependency or addiction.

Men or women who are in touch with their masculinity use the shield when negative criticism is directed at their souls.

For years I used to listen to people tell me what I did wrong after a lecture or a workshop. Vulnerable and scared, I listened to and took their complaints, although I knew I had done the best I could. These people became like the critical father I was raised by, what I call the "four As, one B parent." The kind who focuses on the B on your report card instead of the four As. There's always at least one such parent in a crowd of any size, a person who absolutely must tell me what I did wrong. A few strokes and passes from his tongue and I'd be sliced, diced, and damaged for the day.

Finally, I found my shield and placed it beside me. Now when people come up to me and begin to cut, I grab the shield just as they say, "I loved your lecture or book or workshop, BUT—" My shield goes up and I say, "No, I don't want to hear criticism right now. I'm too shaky and I need your love and support, or nothing at all."

I use my shield when a lover makes me into a parent; when a workshop participant turns me into a father, and it comes down when I feel safe.

For many men—and women as well—the rusting sword stands in the corner, sheathed and seldom drawn. The shield lies hidden under blankets thick with dust; it's almost never dragged out, dusted off, and held up against the bosses, wives, lovers, competitors, or detractors who seek to wound. Most of our fathers never gave us these tools or taught us how to use them.

Men who leave a men's gathering sometimes forget their shields; they go out and tell people about the weekend, what it meant, how it healed them, how it felt to be there. And sometimes those who haven't been to such a gathering and may even feel threatened by one, begin to cut and wound: "It's a return to unbridled wildness and savagery," says one critic. "It's aggressive," says another. "It's not necessary." "Too violent." "Too denigrating to women." They were not there. They did not share the experience. They simply do not understand. But without a shield, a man can undo much of his healing by listening to and taking in such judgments.

The archetypal masculine, whether found in men or women, knows when to swing a sword, raise a shield, protect, say no. They carry both sword and shield with them wherever they go and grieve over any wound they inflict and mourn any loss they suffer. The true masculine is the true warrior who grieves the fact that swords and shields are a necessary part of life, maturity, creativity, caring, and self-love.

## THE NEW MASCULINITY IN ACTION

Men and women want to know what this "new" or "deep" masculinity will look like. Is it just another way for men to form one more elitist and exclusive club, and will it be oppressive to women and children? The answer is a very firm NO.

While I can't say exactly how it's going to be, since we're at the beginning of the process, I can share a few snapshots of this new masculinity in action.

True masculinity in action is the opposite of everything

91

we have been taught. At a gathering when Marvin leads the men through an inner-child exercise, where a man whispers in another man's ear all the things the boy wished he'd heard his father say to him, some cry out in anguish and pain while strong masculine hands reach out to each other. And when Marvin leads one hundred and fifty men around the open pasture in a proud, head-held-high, but not cocky, "King Walk," all present know masculinity can be positive and life-affirming without arrogance and conceit. When two men who have been in a men's group together for several years meet, they embrace, they allow their whole bodies to take in the warmth and support. This is unlike the men who are afraid of such intimacy, due to fears that have been placed inside them by small-minded men.

True masculinity demonstrated by men who are doing their own soul-work is exemplified by people such as Jim R.

Jim and I have known each other for several years. He's been to several men's gatherings and done as much work on himself as any man I've known. I ran into Jim in the airport the other day. His smile walked out in front of him. His embrace came from somewhere deep inside him. He was going to a men's weekend in Georgia with my friend Shepherd Bliss. I was on my way to North Carolina to do a training workshop for therapists.

Once on the plane, we launched into a level of conversation that only feels safe with men who can hear and speak with their guts and hearts. An hour into the flight, I shared with him that although I fly frequently, I was still scared to death most of the time. He listened and said nothing analytical or rational. He just cared. Shortly after telling him about my fears, the plane hit some turbulence unlike any

I've experienced since my first flight on a propeller plane back in 1956 when I was five. The plane rocked and rolled to a rhythm of its own. We bounced up and down and on the second bounce I grabbed Jim's hand and damn near squeezed his fingernails off. He kept smiling at me in a way that said, "I'm here for you," and all he said was, "Keep breathing." I held on and relived that childhood flight full of thunder and lightning and fear. I don't remember my father comforting me.

As I held on, sweat popped out on my forehead, my face went white, and my palms could have watered a small garden. A very nice, well-intentioned man in the aisle seat across from me said, "What's the matter?"

"I'm scared to death," I stuttered.

"There isn't any need to be scared. It'll be over in just a minute. He'll bank out of this and descend to another altitude. Everything will be fine." He looked at my hand hiding in Jim's. "You'll be all right," he added.

"I'm still scared," I said and wiped the sweat. "I appreciate your thoughtfulness." Jim looked at me and once again simply said, "Just breathe."

After the terror subsided I was shaken for several hours afterwards. I thanked Jim for being there for me as we said good-bye in the Atlanta airport. I proceeded to board a propeller plane to shuttle up to North Carolina. As I sat, halfway recovered from the ordeal, I got real sad and joyful at the same moment. Sad because I knew that the man in the aisle across from me was as "well-intentioned" as my dad, and joyful that Jim was well on the way to healing all the bullshit he and I had been taught and hurt by as boys. He was there for me in a way that let me know men are changing.

\* \* \*

Jeffrey is short in stature and carries in him a tall soul and a stout heart. He works in the computer field and has a tattoo that reads, "Death before dishonor" on his right arm. He attended the first men's conference on recovery and codependency, held in Phoenix in 1990. Along with three hundred other men and one hundred women, he wept, danced, and delighted in the energy that the hotel could barely contain, but did. Several months later he attended a men's gathering in Las Vegas, New Mexico, led by Shepherd Bliss, Marvin Allen, and myself. During a break he walked up to me and put that tattooed arm around my neck and said, "Thank you. After that conference in Phoenix, I went home and took my fourteen-year-old son for a long walk. I told him about myself, my childhood, about his grandfather, and I told him how scared I always was to be a man, and how I tried always to be in control of myself, him, and the whole family, because I was so scared. I told him how I hurt, what I dreamed, what I liked and what I didn't. And I finally told him how sorry I was for not being there for him when he was little because I was either at work or "out with the boys" drinking. I made amends to him from my gut with tears in my eyes. He cried, too, and we held each other for a long time. Finally, John, he looked me in the eyes and said, 'Dad, for the first time in my whole life I feel like you really understand me, and that you really know how I feel. I love you, Dad.'"

Jeffrey took a handkerchief from his hip pocket. "I couldn't have done that had I not attended that conference in Phoenix and gotten the support I received there. I told my son that if he'd like to, he could come with me to this gathering, and there he is" (pointing across the field) "putting up our tent. I wish me and my dad could have done something like this."

And then there is Michel. He said to me, "I told Barbara I loved her and liked her, but I needed to be with her in a way that worked for me."

Michel is lean, bearded, and balding. He has a serious Southern drawl and a smile for everyone. He has been for much of his life, in his own words, "a people pleaser."

"I have been in relationships the way others have needed me to be, and I'm tired of it. I can't do what my parents and everybody else says I should do anymore. I don't want to get married. I want to live in my own home, have my friends, grow, change, and heal. I want to be a lover and friend to Barbara, but I don't want to marry her, and I don't want to be pressured to do so just because that's what everybody does who's not 'afraid of commitment.' I want to be me for a change. I want love and to give love, but in a way that feels right for me. Does that make sense to anyone in this group?"

Several men said, "Ho!" a word that many men use at our gatherings to affirm very positively what a man has just said.

Picture this: The new masculinity bringing about a change in language. Imagine these words and phrases disappearing from men's mouths, erased from all their letters pertaining to failed relationships: "Pull yourself up by the bootstraps." "Get back in the saddle." "There's plenty of fish in the sea." "The trouble with you is that you're just too sensitive." Or with regard to work: "If it's worth doing, it's worth doing well." "Working hard? Or hardly working?" "Early to bed, early to rise." "You're wasting daylight." With regard to children: "Oh, they'll get over it. They're resilient." "You don't have to go to the bathroom—you just went." "Big boys don't cry." "Be a 'nice' girl or boy, or Daddy (Mommy) won't like you." "If you don't stop crying, I'll give you something to cry about." "You'll never amount to anything." "You're no son of mine."

Men are at work, as we speak, healing themselves and banishing those words, and others like them.

Brad is about forty, built like a brick wall—thick and hard, but boyish in his face and especially around his eyes. He is employed by the men's center. I walked in the other day and he was sitting at a desk, hiked back, engaged in and apparently enjoying a conversation with one of the therapists who office there. I turned around and walked back to my office, not wanting to interrupt them, thinking to myself, I'm glad they're getting some time together, and getting to know one another. I didn't think any more about it until the next day when Brad knocked on my door, looking quite anxious and a little afraid. "Can I come in? We need to talk." He settled himself on the couch, but couldn't quite sit still. His voice was nervous as he spoke. "Listen, about yesterday—when you came in and saw Rich and me talking—well, I wanted you to know that we'd just started, and I wasn't just killing time. When I saw you turn around and walk off, I thought you thought maybe I was goofing off, and well . . ." I interrupted him. "Whoa, Brad, would you like to even know what I really thought before you go on?" "Sure, but I could tell you were upset and thought I wasn't earning my money." Brad was paid by the hour. "Brad, I thought it was great y'all were getting a chance to spend some time together, and that the more you know about the people who work here, the more comfortable you and they would feel. A large reason I started this place was to bring people together to talk to each other and heal each other." Brad looked embarrassed, yet excited. "God, I forgot that I'm not back at my old job. My old boss would have thought all that stuff, and hell, so would my dad. Back when I worked for him, he just wanted everybody to stay busy and damn near kill themselves. It's hard to get used to the idea that I can be me and not have to be scared of the anger of some man, and always try to second-guess what he's thinking and feeling. Thanks for the support."

Only a father can have such control over a boy's body. Only he can tie a stomach into a knot and make us so scared we can't speak, and make us worry about people and things to the point we imagine all kinds of problems.

The new male will work hard and even hope the people he works with will do a good job. But this old message of "I'm the boss-master, you're the employee-slave" is on the way out. I don't want to be anybody's boss, and I'm damn sure not going to be anybody's slave, nor do I need employee-slaves. What I need is support, sharing, and cooperation.

# THE PRINCESS WITHIN

## Recovering the Feminine

M en come to men's gatherings and men's groups not only to find their masculinity, their fathers, and a fellowship with other men. They are also in search of their feminine side, the Princess within.

Most men are looking outside themselves for the Princess, the perfect feminine. They are looking for a fairy-tale princess in every woman they meet, even though they may have been married for twenty-five years. "Are you my princess, my ideal woman?" "How about you?" "Surely, my secretary must be the one." "I know I'm married, but if I find my ideal, I'll leave my wife." "I've been looking for the Princess all of my life."

Who symbolizes or embodies the Princess for men in this culture? Perhaps Madonna or Princess Diana or Marilyn Monroe. But as one man said at a men's gathering recently, "I can't name many women who are willing to carry the

Princess today. I can think of a lot of men who carry the Prince—Robert Redford, Mel Gibson, Al Pacino, Tom Cruise."

But in order to truly find the Princess, the feminine, the chalice of life, a man must journey into his own interior forest, into his past, and descend into his wounds. And he must do so carefully. A lot of men have moved far away from their own masculinity in their search for the feminine. They may in fact have used the feminine to escape the masculine, if they felt ashamed and frightened of it. They embraced poetry, poverty, and passivity in reaction to the distorted masculinity demonstrated by their fathers. And they found what I've already described as the false feminine, becoming what Robert Bly calls a "soft male." Such men are well-intentioned, but not in touch with true tenderness and a genuine ability to nurture themselves and others. They speak of peace and act complacently, while the planet is destroyed and children are abused. They project their own feminine Princess onto flesh-and-blood women, and when their wives or lovers won't play the game, they pay dearly. They figure they might find another who will play the game, satisfy the illusion.

A man who doesn't find his own interior Princess turns the woman he loves into a witch who eats children for her energy. But in reality his wife may be a mother who has sadly turned to her children for comfort and energy because of the absence of the masculine energy in her husband.

When a man cannot find the Princess, she always appears in his dreams. All her variations and versions visit us at night as we sleep, speaking of feminine messages and mysteries. Some of us awaken and think we've received a message from God to call our ex-girlfriend or wife even though we broke up with her or divorced her ten years ago. We mistake her for our Princess, our feminine, our would-be bride.

When a man gets in touch with his authentic feminine side, his wife or girlfriend or daughter can be who she is, not what he projects upon her. We must court that portion of ourselves that is receptive, slower, darker, wetter, and willing to wait for planted seeds to bear fruit in their own time.

The men's movement is about finding, feeling, and taking back the feminine, while discovering the deep masculine. And ironically men often must gather in men's groups in order to find the feminine. When we're with other men, it is next to impossible to displace the feminine onto anyone else. Many men find her and embrace her among the rocks and trees and grassy knolls in the woods, far away from the pitfalls of the false feminine. As we journey closer to our masculinity, our feminine also becomes our true companion.

## THE FEMININE IN CRISIS

This morning I woke up with these words on my lips, said to no one but myself: "She's not my mother. It's not my crisis. I'm not in crisis because she is. I don't have to fix it." Those words blended with the sunlight streaming through my cabin's window and made me feel better and feel like writing.

The mother is a man's first encounter with the "feminine." The baby boy found the feminine in his mother's face, most assuredly in her eyes. For him the mother/feminine usually meant love, gentleness, tenderness, nurturing, touch, and patience. The boy naturally located his feminine outside himself and placed it on her just as he found his masculine model in his father.

For many men, the feminine is still out there being reflected back to him from some woman's eyes. And for some the fear of losing her is tantamount to losing a part of themselves they've yet to claim. If women pull away, they take that feminine part away with them.

When I was a child, my mother was often in crisis, as she was living with an alcoholic and had been raised by one. Her crises became mine. To the degree that she suffered, I suffered. To the degree that I could feel like I was fixing her by being smart, good, or strong, I increased my chances of getting more of that needed love, tenderness, nurturing that she was more fully able to deliver when she was okay. So my job was to make her, and then, later, other women okay.

After all the work I've done on myself, I sometimes still let my feminine flow out of me and right into a woman. For instance, the other day when my mom, now fifty-nine years old, called in a crisis, within ten minutes her problems were mine and I was "fixing" them at lightning speed. I gave her good suggestions and wrote her a "good" check, and was a "good" son. She was the first feminine and was for me again, after not having been for several years. I felt the "Princess" slip right out of me as I became Mr. Fix-It, her father, her "little man."

I have found that I'm much more able to contain and befriend my feminine side when I'm not in a relationship, or when I'm in a relationship with a woman who is a lot like my father, masculine and unavailable. When this is the case, I'm more like my mom who is very feminine. On the other hand when I'm with a woman who is very feminine, it's more difficult for me not to harness myself to the more traditional role of "the Man."

An example of my willingness to play this role came just last night. My girlfriend called me at my cabin in Alabama saying she wouldn't be able to join me the next day as planned because the man who rents her house called and said the plumbing needed massive repairs or total replacement. In less than five minutes Mr. Fix-It was on the scene making rapid-fire suggestions, quoting Twelve-Step philosophy ("admit we're powerless over plumbing"), and figuring out how she could pay for it all.

This morning I realized that just the other day when I was in a minicrisis all she did was listen attentively and ask what "I needed" from her. I also realized that due to the fact that she'd been absorbed in some deep personal problems the last few weeks, I hadn't been getting much attention, tenderness, or nurturing and that if I didn't fix her problems I might not get any of these things from her for a while longer. Sound familiar?

Today, just as I write these words, I feel my feminine moving back into the rightful owner's body—mine. At this moment I believe I can love myself, be tender toward myself, and give myself what I need. "She's not my mom. It's not my crisis. It's not my fault. I don't have to fix it or her. I'm lovable as I am and I love her enough to make amends, listen, support, and care."

## MEN EMBRACING THE FEMININE WITHIN

Raymond stood up and volunteered to participate in one of the last exercises of the gathering. If we had divided up the men who attended this gathering into clans, this fellow would surely have been comfortable in the Bear Clan. He stood over six feet tall and even growled out his words when he spoke. He was about the size of a medium-sized black bear, with paws for hands, as tender as Gentle Ben.

I'd been talking for an hour or so on how we as men must find our true feminine side as we journey deeper and deeper toward our masculinity. Many of the men had shared how they had let their wives and lovers carry this part of themselves for so long in exchange for their "fathering," "mentoring," and "fixing." Many of the men were deeply grieving because these patterns kept them from being friends to the women they loved. The women in turn had lost touch with their own masculine side, so both parties often sauntered off in search of their missing selves.

I closed the talk with a poem by Ethridge Knight entitled "Belly Song": "She opened to me like a flower, I fell on her like a stone, I fell on her like a stone." The men seemed ready to feel more fully all that had been said and let the metaphors of the "flower" as the feminine and the "stone" as the masculine sink in at a deeper level. I had them imagine that at the heart of each stone grows a flower and at the center of each flower is a stone. I asked who was ready to see the images merge in their own interior world. Several hands went up while Raymond stepped forward. "I'm ready. I need to do this. For myself. My wife and for my children."

I took a stick and drew a circle around him and asked the

men to come in close to support him as we performed a strange kind of ceremony I'd never performed or seen performed prior to that moment. Raymond stood still and dead center of the circle. He closed his eyes. Since I didn't know exactly what I was doing, I got real still inside myself and asked for some kind of guidance. "Raymond, if you're ready, I want you to take several full deep breaths. I want you to picture your mother's face and take her hands very gently in your own and feel her hands and when you're ready tell her good-bye and feel all your feelings as you do so. You're saying good-bye to the mother she was thirty years ago." Raymond started crying. "God, Mom, I got to let you go," he said out loud. "Then picture all the girls and women you've ever loved, one at a time or separately and tell them good-bye. And then picture your wife and your daughters and tell them good-bye for now, but that you'll be seeing them later after this exercise," I said, wondering what the other men's feelings were.

Raymond took a deep breath and huge tears rolled down his cheeks. I continued, "These are the women who you've let carry your own feminine soul over the years. Feel that loss as much as you can. Now I want you to begin feeling that part of yourself that's been out there floating around looking for its rightful home to start very slowly coming into this circle."

Raymond cried and sobbed. His whole body crumpled under the awareness of what he'd done and what he was doing still to the women he loved. This went on ten minutes or more and then he started smiling. "This is weird. While I was crying I could see her standing in this circle facing me and then I swear, it's like something rushed into me and I know it was her. She's the most beautiful woman I've ever seen before in my life. She doesn't look like my wife or my mother or any other of the women I've ever known."

His face glowed in a way that touched every man there. "She's in me. I'll never let her go again, she's the bride I've been searching for all these years. I'll never let her go again. If I do, I'll feel it and do whatever I have to to get her back."

He opened his eyes even though tears were still pouring out of them. "I've never felt this good before. Having her here inside me" (pointing at his heart) "makes me feel better than any drug or woman ever did. Thanks, guys."

He looked around and into the faces of over one hundred and thirty men, and finally said, "I sure could use a hug."

Raymond called me a couple of months ago. "My wife and I are closer than ever. We support each other in ways we never have before. And ever since that gathering, I know this sounds weird, but I let her drive more, and I spend lots more time cooking.

## LETTER TO A PARTNER

Dear Woman:

This weekend I touched the feminine. I let that part of me that slips into my dreams in a variety of forms and with many faces actually become real inside me. I, who live so much of the time in my head and who call upon the masculine to move mountains, build bridges, and pay bills, have longed for this interior female that all men possess but usually abandon and project onto women.

Perhaps the reason we're together is because you're so

feminine so much of the time. You, with your oceanic waves of feeling and spontaneity and sensuality, encourage me on good days; confuse me on bad ones. Your sexuality, like your soul, does not punch in and out on company time-cards or live by clocks and calendars, but rather exists in seasons and cycles and rhythms that I came to know deeply this weekend for a little while, as I have on a few other occasions.

So you see, one of the reasons I've sometimes recoiled from your touch and sunk into sadness is that I've been afraid I would lose the feminine I'd found for brief moments. I feared that you would carry that function for me. I was scared that there wouldn't be enough room in this three-bedroom, two-bath house for my feminine side, and yours.

My interior feminine inhabits my home so rarely that I was afraid she'd disappear in your presence, in the same way as your masculine side sometimes moves out of my way.

Another reason I often can't look at you as lovingly as I feel is that I grew up with a "devouring mother," who was very feminine and ate my masculine energy on the days Dad provided none. She made no room in our house for my feminine side and my father—who let my mother carry that energy for him—certainly did not encourage me to develop my femininity.

So you see, it's not that I don't love you, and it's not that I'll always feel this afraid. But you must understand that my healing depends so much on my ability to hold onto my feminine side and still be in your presence. I'm learning how to do just that, but I must go slowly. I wrote this letter because I know about my fear of losing my femininity, which I only just found. I wanted you to know that I'm determined to find more of her over the coming years. And I wanted you to know that I hope this process will bring me closer to you.

P.S. I know you're not my mother.

# COMING DOWN OFF THE MOUNTAIN

## Taking the Journey into Everyday Life

"Coming down off the mountain, I can't find
anyone who wants to dance around a fire at
midnight."

Jeff, after a men's gathering

I t's Sunday night and the weekend's over. I'm sure the men walking toward their cars feel much like the men who left after a week-long men's gathering on top of Rose Mountain in New Mexico led by my friend and partner Dan Jones. The weekend on Marvin's ranch had been so good and so intense that coming back to the city was not only difficult but at times downright depressing.

Men who leave a men's gathering, or even a two-hour men's group, sometimes feel confused and frustrated by the fact that they can't seem to carry what they've learned or felt back to their families, jobs, or friendships. On the mountain, at the meeting, on the weekend retreat, they are with men totally committed to being there and being open. When they return to their lives, they find the same people and the same old pitfalls.

People involved in any form of recovery that engages them fully will know what I mean. When the men come off the mountain, they carry with them a glowing fire. They are often very committed to their own healing and want desperately for their lives to accommodate this new commitment. They want everyone to be warmed, see the light, and hear their prayer. Most can't. Their families and friends weren't there and many will never choose to be. So after the days of celebration and damage-repair are over, and the descent is made into the city, the dysfunctional workplace, and the codependent relationship, some men ask themselves several questions: "Was what I did real?" "Why can't I feel that way all of the time?" "Why can't my wife and children experience my joy?" "Why can't my boss go to one of these things?" "Why didn't my dad ever do this? Why won't he now?" And when a man tells someone who was not there about the drumming, the sweat lodge, or the tears, it is very likely that she or he will not understand.

Men come down off the mountain or out of the weekend with their shields down, their hearts open, wanting to tear down walls between themselves and others. And they go back to a boss who could not care less, a girlfriend who has not made a similar commitment to recovery, or a father who shames him for not being able to handle his problems "on his own." And the men wonder why the mountain doesn't stay with them in their muscles, memories, or manhood.

When I return from a men's gathering, I still want to dance around glowing fires and beat drums into the night. I can't help but notice that no one in town is building any fires, and the dances they do I don't much understand. And I know that the fire and the dance must be experienced inside me and I must seek out the support of those who know, who've been there. I feel like Rilke when he wrote, "I want to be with those who know secret things or else alone." I have to trust that after a while I can integrate my experience and let its memory help shape my character and enhance the quality of my relationships. But to ensure that this happens and to support me in the meantime, it's important to be with safe people with whom I can share and grow. For not until we're with people who are actively healing can we return to the mountain. Until a man has learned a lot more about shields and swords, and realized the difference between walls and boundaries, he will fall into his old traps. And such lessons cannot be learned in one weekend or week. A lot of recovery time is needed before unhealthy people and situations stop affecting him. In the meantime he needs to be patient with those who choose to stay behind. And he needs to be sure to spend time with those who know what he knows. He may even need to use his newly found sword to cut harmful, nonsupportive people and circumstances out of his life.

A few years ago I broke off a relationship with a woman whom I loved very much. I'd known her for a very long time, and it was one of the hardest things I've ever done, almost as difficult as the time I chose not to see my mother and my father for a while.

As much as I loved Linda, as much as she loved me, as much as she said she was committed to healing, an abyss separated us. The abyss was not in her mind but in mine. She seemed unwilling to descend into her own wounds and wrestle with her own issues, and thus kept projecting many of them on me and others close to her. At that stage in my recovery—and to this day—I needed to put my healing before anything or anybody else. I had hurt myself and hurt too many others for too long by people-pleasing, giving up, and putting out. I wanted to know that the person I was with would not allow me, work, money, or even a child to come between herself and her own healing. If a person is not committed to herself then how can she be truly committed to me? I had to let Linda go. God, how I hurt, how she hurt. And yet I healed at a level I never thought possible. Nearly a year later, after the grief subsided, I met a woman who loved herself enough to make recovery number one. And I feel safe enough to tell her anything, even safe enough to let the fire be lit and the dance begin.

## A SAFE PLACE FOR SOUL-WORK

Other than the mountaintop, only a few places in the world are safe enough for a man to feel the loss of his father, the loss of a job, the severing of a relationship, the hole he carries in his soul. One of those places is a men's group structured around "soul-work." The confrontation and competition that goes on in some groups serve only to camouflage the real issues men must face and feel. In a soul-work group, safety must prevail because when we were boys the few times we did open our souls to someone we were bruised and hurt. Men must feel supported to go down into those places and pull out their pain and place it before other men.

This is very difficult. When men enter a men's group they wonder if the men are going to tell the truth—so many men have lied to them including their fathers. Are the men leading the group working on themselves? So many therapists don't. Are the facilitators going to tell them what to do and how to do it? So many men are very ready to tell other men what to do. Are the other fellows there going to run away when they tell the secrets that have shamed them for decades? Will the men who gather around to listen, laugh, or ridicule them like their fathers often did? They wonder if they do start crying over all their losses and hurts if they'll ever stop. They worry about taking up too much time because their pain is "so much less" then they perceive others have in them. They're afraid that they will disappear if they deal with their dads.

My partner Dan works on himself every week in some way and sits like Buddha in the flesh, full of human foibles and frailties like the rest of us, but full of compassion for what these men are going through. He loves them. They love him. Dan and I grow together like two separate but equal strands of ivy merging and then going off in separate directions. We sometimes finish each other's thoughts and sentences like some old couple who has been together for a lifetime.

Together we watch men descend, slowly at first. We wait patiently as men make the longest journey they'll ever make—the seventeen inches from their heads to their hearts. And with time, those men become models to the new guys in the group afraid of working on their stuff in front of men. And I grow every time we meet together and I love each one there. After six years of being with many of those men who started out as "clients," I watch as they turn into my brothers and people who give to me as much, if not more, than I to them.

Each man in the group is afraid. Each of us as leaders of men's groups is afraid. The fears decrease as the trust in other men increases through time and patience. A safe men's support group can become the net one jumps into when leaving the mountain. Either way, the gatherings are good beginnings, and the group is where the soul and the body deepen their recovery.

# PART THREE

# THE HEALING

# MUSIC TO FIND
# OUR FATHERS BY

"Rhythm and noise. There is terror in noise, and in that
terror there is also power.

Mickey Hart

Some of the drums make low sounds like distant thunder that rolls right into my chest. Others make sounds that are shrill, as did the lard cans I drummed on when I was a kid. There are as many different drums as there are men: African drums, homemade drums, bongos, congas, big-band drums, and a few tambourines. They're played by hands that only days before were selling stocks, punching time cards, extracting teeth, or hurling garbage cans.

The drumming begins each weekend or week-long rebirthing, as the men who are already there greet those arriving with sounds that are at first hesitant, awkward, and cacophonous. Most of the men, not having drummed since grade school, wonder what good will come out of it. At first, they cannot find a beat that is natural to them. As the beating becomes very fast and rushed like the rhythms of the cities so many of them just left, they wonder how drums can heal.

But a few hours into the weekend the drums become—as they always have been—a source of power and energy for the men who open themselves to the sounds. The drum is the best instrument I know for breaking down walls and catapulting primal pain up and out, booming into an evening sky.

As the weekend moves from its beginning to its middle, the drumming becomes more proficient. The beats slow down and become rich and deep. Men move from a disorganized pounding herd to a tightly knit clan that knows when to begin and exactly when to end. The men still can't say why they are drumming, but more and more often they do say, "Let's drum" when something powerful or moving has been shared.

By the end of the weekend, the drumming, once discordant, has become a thundering symphony that we dance to and delight in and use when words just aren't good enough. By the time we say good-bye, the sounds of the drums have helped heal some of our souls' sickness and begun to close the gap between fathers and sons, mothers and sons, men and men, men and women. Many of the men describe the synchronized drumbeats as signifying that life is worth living and the earth belongs to all men, women, and crawling, flying, swimming, and walking beings.

At night when I go to sleep, I hear the drums pounding in my ears, and it's hard to tell if they are echoes from the day or if men are still up and in the grove at 2:00 A.M., celebrating to the sounds of a thunder drum. I can feel the drumbeat reverberating through me now as I write, and I'm thankful to people like Mickey Hart, Michael Meade, and Michael Harner who have helped put the drums back into the healing process and back into my body.

# THE FATHER QUEST

## Letting Go of Dad

The drums link men to their masculine heritage. They produce a sound chain connecting us to our father, his father's father, all the way back through generations of men. This merger with the deep masculine helps men find the courage to confront their fathers' ghosts.

"He's standing behind that tree—see? Look real quick. He just ducked back. Now he's behind that rock. Your father is out there and he can't join us. He would if he could, but he can't. You have to go out there yourself and find him. Draw a circle large enough for both of you and make him come in and sit down. Then ask him to be silent and listen to you while you tell him all the things you always wanted to say but that he couldn't or wouldn't take the time to hear. Do what you have to do to entice him into that circle and don't let him out until you say he can leave."

Marvin Allen and I provide the instructions for the counter, and the men provide the deep desire, the fear, and the courage to continue the quest they've been on, albeit unconsciously, for decades. This is an exercise we call the "father quest."

"Some of you may need to pick up a stick or a limb and you may have to slap it hard against the ground to get his attention. And some of you may have to use it symbolically on him as a way to release your rage about all the times he used something on you to get your attention: the belts, the switches, the silence.

"Now some of you may need simply to weep while your father watches and some of you may want to tell him how much you missed him, how much he missed, how much he meant," I say in a low voice.

"Whatever you have to do or say is okay and you have our support," Marvin says.

The men move slowly out into the woods, onto the rocks, out into the open places and draw their circles. Some are cautious at first: others engage the ghost father immediately and the talking, shouting, moaning, crying, and pounding begin. Nothing is more touching to me than watching men perform this ritual. They are finally choosing to take the rage out of their bodies and put it onto the real object of their fury instead of onto another or back onto themselves. Men are scattered in all directions, but they are all focusing on the father they never had, never felt, but never forgot.

After about half an hour of making contact with their wounds, the warriors return to the circle and begin to drum, allowing the sounds and motions to release any distress that is left—an emotion that will be returned to later. The drum-beat is like a bandage that wraps the places still bleeding. The beat is not a dirge for Dad, but a celebratory sound that sings, "I'm finally feeling and healing and genuinely moving toward real forgiveness for a father who could never do this himself."

## STOP SONNING

A forty-year-old man named Jason told the men gathered around him how he spoke one night on the phone to his father. He was "sonning" up a storm, and his father was fathering in the only way he ever knew how. "Sonning" is a term Dr. Joseph Cruse uses to describe how men perform the role of a son without even realizing it; a role that turns men into little boys. When men act like sons, their parents act in kind, and men get pissed off, frustrated, and end up feeling small. Perhaps more importantly, if men are still "sonning" with their parents, they're sure to be doing the same with wives or lovers, leading to dysfunction that can rival that of their childhood.

Jason had been reduced to rageful tears several times in his weekly men's group, remembering how his father had never listened to him when he expressed his emotions, how he had only wanted Jason to achieve, not grow or feel. One night, Jason decided to call his dad: he wanted to share what he'd learned with his father, and to tell him about the men's gatherings he'd attended. He needed his dad to hear him.

"Well, that sounds fine, son. I'm sure it was worth the

time and money you spent. How's your new job going these days?"

His father's patronizing tone and lack of interest put Jason right back where he was before all his work; at least for the moment, he became a son seeking the approval of a father who couldn't give it twenty-five years ago and still can't.

As Jason told us how much he had wanted his father to listen, he looked at me with eyes as sad as anyone's I've ever seen and said, "I've even got to let him go at this level, too, don't I? I have to let my dad go, don't I?"

At that instant, I could feel that Jason was finally willing to stop sonning, and he joined the ever-increasing group of men who are no longer willing to act on their need for fathering or mothering from their parents. I then asked Jason to tell his father how he felt now. And this is what he said:

"Dad, I'll always be your son and you'll always be my father, but I don't need parenting by you anymore. I need to stop sonning you. I need you to talk to me like an adult you respect and appreciate. I don't need your money, your advice, your shaming, your criticizing, or for you to ignore my boundaries. I need to treat you like someone who I love and share a great deal of history with. But I need to forge a new relationship with you and I need for you to be willing to try to be my friend as I am willing to try to listen to you and speak my truth even if it hurts you to hear it.

"I don't expect us to master this new mode of being overnight. I know that after thirty-nine years I'll slip back from time to time and act thirteen with you, and I know you all will act like it's 1960 instead of 1990. But I do expect you to be willing to try with me. And if you should choose not to try, then we will not be able to be close for a while. I refuse to son you. I would rather not talk to you at all. I know this will be awkward and difficult for a while, but I need to let you go. I've felt anger and grief at the way I was fathered, and I'm sure I'll feel some more from time to time. But I can tell it's time to let you go and to say, 'Stop fathering. I'm going to stop sonning.'"

Jason and his father are now sending cassette tapes back and forth every month or so. They have agreed to use this medium as a way to really show each other who they are now. They're trying to become friends.

## ATONING

Sometimes a middle-aged or older man will walk up to me near the end of a gathering or conference: He's always solemn with shoulders bent slightly toward the ground, as if weighted down with guilt.

"A lot of what you talked about this weekend I've done to my children. I haven't been there for them. I whipped them, shamed them. I did what was done to me. How can I ever make that up to them? How can I right the wrongs?"

My answer is always, "You will when you're ready, when you want to in your gut, not just in your head." These men need to wait until it really feels right, for a time when they won't want something in return. For a time when they are doing it for their healing and not their kids'. They have to love themselves enough to be forgiven and they must be ready to forgive themselves. Then and only then should

124

they go to their children whether they are two, ten, or forty, and take their faces gently in hand and look them in the eyes and say, "Please forgive me. I apologize for hurting you. I'm sorry. I love you."

And I tell these men to expect nothing afterward except to feel better. Don't expect to receive their forgiveness, don't expect that they will even take in what you've said; and certainly don't expect the apology to erase their mistakes, the divorce, the anger, or the fear. You won't be saving them from doing work on themselves; you can't heal their wounds, even if you were largely responsible for inflicting them. If this is your motive, they'll know it; and they'll sense that you're just being inauthentic and controlling one more time.

But do expect that at some level and at some point, it will make a difference in their lives. Think about it: Had your father ever come to you sincerely asking for forgiveness, what would you have done? What would you have felt? Would your wounds be as deep and painful as they are today?

And imagine that when I ask an audience twenty years from now, "How many of you had parents who worked on themselves while you were growing up; how many of you had a father who came to you and made amends?" Your kids will raise their hands, and the time it takes them to heal will be cut in half.

But your dad didn't ask. More than likely he never will. He's probably still in denial about your pain and his. All you can do is begin forgiving yourself and letting go of the need for him to get up out of the grave or crawl out of the bottle or put down the newspaper or turn off the TV and come ask for your forgiveness. It's probably not going to happen.

But you know that you are grieving and getting angry and getting on with your life. And your children or nieces or nephews or grandchildren are watching you as you heal. You might just end up being their island of sanity in a sea of family chaos. Remember that you're doing good work.

## · MENTORING

Young men, old men, men in the middle are almost all in need of a mentor. A mentor is a man or for a woman, it's a woman, who can teach, encourage, hold up a lamp during a dark time, model, and make meaning out of chaos.

Most men have never had a mentor, or what Robert Bly calls a "male mother." They've never had someone who helps nurture their talents and encourages them to pursue their passions. The mentor's role is not that of a father or a therapist; a mentor does not feel or heal the younger man's pain, he is there to stimulate his curiosity and provide information and share experiences.

Wayne Kritsberg sat down with me years ago after having read my first book, *The Flying Boy*. He recommended it to his publisher and told me some of the things I could expect from being on the road, and how much to charge as a speaker. He very carefully and noncompetitively guided me through a process that would have been overwhelming were it not for his information.

Bill Stott, now a coauthor of two of my books, mentored me in the writing process. For years he would read the words I'd string together in less-than-artful ways, and comment on them in constructive, rather than critical ways. He was supportive of me during those early years when I had little confidence or ability to support myself. He shared every secret with me he knew about good writing. He shared parts of himself and his history that I could relate to and use.

But a man who has not let his father go, a man who has not stopped being a son will misuse his mentor; he'll feel abandoned when his mentor doesn't spend as much time with him as he'd like, or return his phone calls as quickly as he wants him to. A man still clinging to the father he never had and always wanted will project his unfulfilled needs onto his mentor.

Men must not expect their mentors to be anything but the flesh and blood that they are. Mentors can't and shouldn't be our daddies or saints or saviors. The mentor you select is only too human and is probably still healing his own wounds and recovering at his own pace, just as we are.

We cannot forget that we need the mentor's words, his art, his wisdom, his knowledge, although we have no right to them. If he gives, we are privileged and should be honored. If he withdraws from us, we can only grieve—never demand.

There probably will come a time when we'll have to let our mentors go. Indeed, if the ones we choose are healthy, they will gently push us out on our own. And if they are really healthy, and if time and circumstances allow, they will want to cultivate a new relationship—as a peer or a good friend. But we can't be either unless we heal our father-son wound enough to let our mentors go, and allow ourselves to see ourselves as their equals, all the while still appreciating them and respecting them for who they are and how they helped.

I hope older men (not necessarily in years but in experience), whether in recovery or drumming or accounting or doctoring, will become willing to mentor other men. And I hope men who have stopped "sonning" will start asking men to be their mentors knowing they may get noes from some, maybe from many. But someone will eventually come into their life and say yes.

# BECOMING YOUR OWN FATHER

## The Art of Re-Parenting

Once men tear down their walls, drop their addictions, grieve, take back their power and their projections, they will be able to father themselves. Some men have a long way to go before they can begin to parent themselves—or anyone else. They're not ready to let go of their fathers' hands. As long as they have begun the letting-go process, it's okay to let go at their own good time.

But many men *are* ready to embrace the practice of re-parenting and incorporate it into their everyday lives. Some men may have sons and daughters who are re-parenting themselves. I hope these dads are proud of them. Still others are learning to stop sonning while teaching their adult kids to do the same. Parents who can't let their children go almost always raise children who can't let their parents go. Thousands of us are finally learning what the Twelve-Step program of Al-Anon has taught for decades: the process of letting go with love. We're also learning what Adult Children of Alcoholics call becoming your own parent.

## THE INNER FATHER

As we let go more and more of the father who rules our behavior and bodies we find an "inner father" who has always been in us, waiting to be recognized. Just as there is an inner child, so too there is an inner old man. Some men who grew up hating the word "father" may resist calling this being inside them "Father." So call him whatever you like—you can even call him Al.

Having done so much rage- and grief-work around my own father, I feel like calling him the "good father," thus distinguishing him from the other "negative father" that still struggles to stay alive and in control.

After I broke up with my girlfriend a few years ago, it took weeks before I could silence the negative criticism my introjected negative father (the father who lives in my brain) bombarded me with on a daily basis.

"Boy, you can't do anything right. You'd think by now you'd either get it right or give up and let somebody who could, do it and get out of their way. You're a joke. Giving workshops, writing books on relationships. You better get a real job . . ."

This voice used to take over after every lecture and workshop: "You forgot to talk about . . . You spent too much time on . . . You used really poor grammar . . . You didn't explain . . ."

I had to do some deep release work to get that parent out of me. I sat down and told myself regarding the relationship breakup: "Look, you did the best you could. You'll do better next time. You'll get some more tools, information, and time in recovery. You're a loving man and you deserve a healthy, loving relationship." I now have a good inner father to throw up a shield in my behalf.

I imagine the good father to be like a loyal warrior. He guards the kingdom wherein lives the inner child, son of the king. Sometimes the king can protect the holy child. Sometimes the king needs protection himself. The good father warrior moves in front of the arrows that come from many directions.

The man who is still beating himself for his mistakes is letting the negative father rule his kingdom. The man who allows this will beat his own children, perhaps not physically, but emotionally. Beating oneself is not equivalent to taking responsibility for oneself and one's actions. The inner father that loves us no matter what we do, what we accomplish, what we don't, what we become, what we don't, is the father we wanted to have in the flesh. This father is an energy, an archetype, a steady, sturdy presence that exists in our bones, blood, psyches, and souls. He can be spoken to. We can ask him questions. He speaks to us in different ways. Sometimes through other people, sometimes through Twelve-Step meetings, men's groups, books, or with a very strong but gentle voice when we're quiet enough and still enough to listen. You'll know this voice. It never shames. It never criticizes, demeans, preaches, or patronizes. It polishes and shines you as if you were a rare coin; as if you were the only one-of-a-kind—which you are. It supports you. It unconditionally loves you for simply showing up on the planet. It guides rather than rules. It tells you to rest rather than "get your lazy ass out of bed and get to work." It tells you to love yourself, your family, and friends more than money.

Finding our inner father, letting go of the flesh-and-blood dad, lets us stop blaming him, puts the responsibility for healing on us, rather than waiting for him to change, and gently nudges us into manhood. When the voice of the inner father is heard more often, we're on our way to loving ourselves, nature, other people, and God.


## ANSWERING A FATHER'S CALL

Today it is quiet. It wants to rain but can't, so it just sprinkles. Some days my crying is like that.

Yesterday, after returning from a lecture and workshop in Washington, D.C., I checked my message machine and to my surprise, my father had called. We haven't spoken but once in three years and then only for a moment, since he was drinking and I chose not to talk to the alcohol that controlled his tongue. It was clear from his message that he was sober and very sad. He said he loved me and wished things were different. He said he was proud of me.

Now I know I need this silence so I can go down into my feelings about my father's phone call. I could get up right now and change my clothes and my disposition by going to the office. There I could successfully numb the pain and not have to probe for and ponder feelings that are sometimes still difficult to find. I could drown myself in the problems of others and the processes that keep other men, and women, from feeling. Today I'm taking the day off.

I need to rest and be still to treat solitude like a guest I'm trying to befriend, instead of the foe my father taught me it was. My dad and mom could never sit still and just be. When Dad came in from his job, he went right to work on his yard, his car, or the latest gadget he'd bought with over-time pay. He'd work until it was dark or time to eat. He'd read the newspaper until he fell asleep. And Mom, also, never missed a beat, working long into the night, washing dishes, cleaning, and caretaking. By the time I was twenty, I could work seventy-hour-weeks and be proud of myself. After years of recovery and therapy, it is much easier to be with myself and my feelings.

Most men, pressured to produce, practice the fine art of avoiding their emotions by staying forever busy. Men, especially those over thirty grew up believing their parents' teaching: "It is noble to work oneself into the ground for pay, and play is something you do when you're a child or with alcohol on your breath. An idle mind and idle hands are the devil's playground."

I'm glad my dad called. I'm glad I don't have to go to work today. I know how to work hard, but I'm learning how to find my feelings and how to say "no" to the way my father and mother worked. As I just sit here and listen to the sound of planes above my head and birds in the backyard, I hear my breath leave my body and come back in again. I feel . . . what . . . I don't know just now . . . but I feel. I-put-down-my-pen-and-just-feel . . .

# REACHING OUT

## Men Supporting Other Men

One of the most important things that happens at men's gatherings is that men get the opportunity to touch and be touched in nurturing and supportive ways. This is not a touchy-feely thing like some of the encounter groups of the sixties and seventies, but a respectful reaching out.

When we hold out our hands to another man or take him in our arms to be held, he will most likely feel the father's hands he never held reaching through time and space. When a man touches another man this way, he is almost always afraid, sad, angry, and joyful all in the same moment. He's afraid he'll be hurt again, abandoned against his will; he's afraid to trust that another man could really be there for him—no strings attached. He's sad because in another man's arms, he asks himself, "Why has this been so long in coming? Why have thirty or forty or fifty years been lived without the opportunity to cry on another man's shoulders?" He's sad that he probably taught his own sons and daughters that men can't really be trusted, and he's angry that his culture sees two men crying and holding each other and thinks, "There's something wrong with a man who'll let another man see him cry, let alone hold him while he does so." He's angry about all the misunderstandings and guilt attached to longing for the nonsexual comfort of another man's touch.

And lastly, he's joyful that he finally put himself in a position where he's safe enough to experience and express his emotions in the company of men. He's joyful that even though he's waited decades, he didn't die with all that grief buried, hidden deep inside. He's joyful that he didn't do what his dad did and just pretend he didn't need support from other men. He may even feel ecstasy that he is healing along with other men who want to do the same.

In a workshop recently, Robert was letting tears roll down his face as I said, "Men want and need to be held by other men in a nonsexual but nurturing manner."

Robert's head bobbed up and down with each word. "Would somebody come up here and try something with me?" I asked a crowd of two hundred men, although I was looking directly at Robert. He immediately raised his hand.

I sat down on one of the bales of hay we had surrounding the fire. I slapped my knee. "Hop up here." Without a moment's hesitation, he came up and sat on my lap. And as soon as I put my arms around him, he began to weep. This six-foot, three-inch bearded man who runs his own landscaping company cried like a four-year-old.

Most of the men who watched were realizing that they, too, had wished and waited for a turn that never came from their fathers, uncles, or big brothers. Many of them cried as well. Undoubtedly most of them had wanted thousands of times in their lives for someone other than a wife or a lover or a mother to hold them.

Women know the men they love need physical attention even if the men themselves are still unsure or unconvinced. Women know this because they also need physical affection from their own sex, only they've had the ability to ask for support for a long time. It's quite common for women to seek refuge in the arms of other women. They know how much it will help; they feel the benefits.

Men were taught that if they wanted arms of the same sex to hold them, there was something deeply defective in them. There isn't. There never was. But there is a lot of pain that gets eased and wounds that get healed a bit when a man can let another man hold him.

"How does that feel?" I asked Robert as his tears were subsiding. "Great. I feel great." "Then get up and let me have a turn," I said. We hugged, and I sat in his lap for a few minutes.

## BEING THERE FOR FRIENDS

This morning I saw a hummingbird sitting still, slowly drinking from a fountain. I'd never seen a hummingbird up close that wasn't flapping furiously and darting from flower to flower.

I have two friends I've known for years. I love them like brothers. I've spent lots of time with them and I've seldom seen them be still. They both fly from their bodies, and their woundedness while reading everything about healing they can get their hands on. One even tries all kinds of therapy and new-age healing strategies for about a month and then moves on to the next latest craze or fad. The other tries nothing, believing nothing could really help him.

I've known each for about eleven years and I've watched their minds grow. I've also witnessed their emotional bodies within seemingly become smaller. It's hard for me to be around either of them for very long for the sound of flapping wings, theirs as well as mine, gets loud and tiring. My emotional body is still small and my readiness to get in my head is great, and I'm still capable of flying away from my feelings.

With one friend, as soon as we get together we either start talking about business, projects, payroll, or people. With the other, it's politics, philosophy, the media, or the mess the planet's in. In other words: shortly after we greet each other with hugs, we head for our heads and we hide there until we say good-bye.

I have two other friends. I've known them for about as long and love them more than I can say. One's emotional body grows each year. He works on it. He nurtures it regularly. He doesn't push himself or me to pump it up. It's just that he wants to feel as well as think. He's not afraid to descend into the pain and wounds, thus he's very comfortable with me should I need to do so in his presence.

He and I talk about some of the same things my other friends and I do, but we also share parts of our souls with the other at a level that I've seldom seen men do. With him I can cry, grieve, get angry, and be a recovering adult child of an alcoholic who is recovering his masculinity while being a man who is sometimes sad or joyful, in grief or in good times. This is why I choose to spend my most difficult times of the year, like Christmas holidays, with him. He shares my feelings about the insanity of the holiday, and by being able to express his feelings appropriately, provides a safety to enjoy the sacred parts of the holiday, which for me includes the celebration of friendship.

The other safe friend also steadily works on himself and goes to men's groups and gatherings. We go to Twelve-Step meetings and meet once a week to share a meal and our souls with each other. He is both gentle and sturdy, and his emotions are within reach. He moves from his head to his heart just as if there were no difficulty in the journey. When he gives me a hug, I can feel his joy and his sorrow reaching out to mine to be embraced and fully felt.

I look at the two men who've completely engaged themselves in their healing processes, and these men go deeper into themselves and are capable of going deeper with other men and the women they love. The first two men and I have reached a level of intimacy that at least for now is as deep as they can go. It makes me sad to see us be so superficial in our love. Though we can't go deeper I still love them just as much. But I don't feel as safe to be with them for extended periods, and when I leave I'm always aware they are mirrors for me, and remind me of the work I need to do. I leave longing for greater closeness and intimacy as I did when my father and I would say good-bye after a visit where two souls would seldom touch.

I used to try to counsel these two men and my father. Now I try just to love them and I don't expect them to give what they can't. I try to stay in my body while I'm in their presence, but it's hard for me because I've lived a long time in the area between my ears, and still stay there more than I'd like to. I know they are exactly where they're supposed to be in their own processes, and like the hummingbird, they'll stop one day and be still. I'll see them and feel their growing emotional bodies, and will have a talk from the heart instead of the head. We'll grieve together for all the time spent in less than satisfying ways, and make up for lost time by really listening and saying things that not only make sense, but heal wounded souls as well.

# THE SEASONS OF A MAN'S LIFE

## Ritual and Grieving

ometimes in the hottest part of the day in the middle
of a dry, seemingly eternal Texas summer, there's
a moment when thoughts and even feelings of fall
are present. Right smack-dab in the midst of the saddest
moments is a pinhole of joy. And in the joy, at its very
center, is sadness. At the center of each season of a man's
life is buried and hidden another season. In the wrinkled
baby's face you can see, if you look closely enough, the
wisdom of the elderly. And in the aged face of an eighty-
year-old man, you can catch the occasional glimmer of the
baby's innocence. The adolescent boy awkwardly stands
facing his midlife crisis and doesn't know it or care. But
midlife is there waiting if he survives his teens and tumul-
tuous twenties.

What follows are some thoughts, feelings, and a few
facts about the seasons of a man's life.

Our society provides almost no recognition to how men (or women) pass through time. It provides very little support for the aging process that we all go through. Without such guidelines, some men in this country are old before their time; and some never grow up. Others weave in and out of life's lanes like a drunk driver waiting to be pulled over and finally arrested for "not knowing" how to be a man. Men in general don't know how to age gracefully, and they don't know when to let go. They don't know about the ancient Eskimo who sat on the ice and cut it away from his tribe, sailing into the snowy silence because it was time, because he knew the season.

We have four seasons: childhood, adolescence, young adulthood, and finally old-age. Each season not observed, each not lived, not grieved and let go of, will cause the heart to attack itself, the back to ache, the shoulders to sag, and serenity to disappear. As we must re-member the body, so, too, we must respond to the seasons, and honor them by speaking about them, feeling them, understanding them, and finally accepting their passing, and therefore ourselves.

## GREETING MY FORTIES

By the time you read this, I'll be forty or older. Some men are so scared to see a four beside a zero that they go into shock and denial and use a number of numbing agents to soften their entrance into the second half of life. Some call this middle-age madness or mindless middle-age crazies.

One of the many reasons forty is so hard on men, even though most are ever so silent on the subject, is, once again, due to our inability to grieve. And one of the things we most hate to acknowledge is the loss of lust, the loss of body parts and body functions. Yet this is the most important loss we suffer during this season of our life. And it must be grieved.

Men like to be noticed by women, especially young women. You can call it vanity or ego, but a more fitting word would be natural. We all like to be looked at, admired, and found pleasing to the eye.

When I was a young college professor in my early thirties, ages nineteen to twenty-four seemed awfully young; yet to receive a glance, a stare, or occasional wink from a woman in this age range didn't wound me any, I can promise you.

During the years before I began my recovery, before semisanity was achieved, I used to act on the occasional come-on from younger women, as long as they weren't students. Either that or lust led to a rich sexual fantasy played out on my mental screen.

The other day, a young, gorgeous woman in her middle twenties, and in her most revealing bikini, looked at me in a way I haven't been looked at in years. Every man and woman nearby saw her. I wanted to ask each to sign an affidavit to this effect for a keepsake. My friend Jim, who was standing nearby, nearly swallowed his tongue trying to get the words out, "Who is sh-sh-she? Did you see the way she looked at you?"

Four things happened: (1) I was flattered and thankful for a thorough eyeballing. (2) I instantly became a little frustrated and more than curious as to why now, of all times, she singled me out. (3) I was amazed that my need to act out my lust was at such a low level that I merely spoke a gentle and thankful "hello" and smiled back. (4) I grieved the loss of my lust and accepted my middle-agedness with more dignity and grace than I ever thought I could muster back when I was thirty. And the grieving that went on that day and part of the next helped me more fully let go of my twenties, my thirties, and the behaviors that went along with them—the restlessness, the cravings, and the loneliness.

With each decade, loss passes over a man's body, painting lines around his eyes, adding inches to his waistline, and a slight sag to those ever-narrowing shoulders. Unless a man grieves each change, each passing, he cannot fully enter into the present. He'll always be teased and tugged by the past.

The other day, I had a tooth pulled. The pain of the extraction was almost nonexistent and yet that evening I looked at the tooth and wept. There was a hole in my mouth where a part of me used to be and will never be again. A part of my body is gone. This may sound small, but to me it is highly symbolic and foreshadows the decades to come. I feel grief over a tooth, a hole that is left, a youth that is quickly disappearing.

I looked in the mirror while at my health club the other day. I was sitting at an angle and in a position that showed a chest that at first I thought couldn't be mine. It had to belong to my father or grandfather. It was wrinkled and folded like a sheet of cloth that could only be seen as not new. The sadness rose up through my folded chest and ran out my eyes for a single moment.

Grieving the hole left by departed lust, the hole left by an extracted tooth, the chest that is slightly wrinkled and folded, leaves me plenty of room for a beautiful vivacious, sensual, sexy, smart woman, and leaves me able to enter my fifth decade with expectancy, exuberance, and energy.

The energy I would have used to deny these feelings is free to feel and be. As I bid these decades farewell, I stand on the brink of a second half and shout "hello," knowing that even if no one returns my greeting, my echo will go on forever and continue to circle back and greet me again and again.

## RECLAIMING AND HONORING THE OLDER MAN: PICTURES FROM MEETINGS AND GATHERINGS

Jim arrived at the gathering early Friday afternoon. His spirits were high and his father was by his side. Jim had been in therapy for about four months. He was twenty-four. His father had never been in therapy or a support group, and he was sixty-five years old. Neither he nor his son, had ever been to a men's gathering before.

Mr. Waitman stood in stark contrast to his son. Jim was full-bodied, golden-haired, blue-eyed, and distant. Mr. Waitman was slender and bent by time and responsibility. His hair was gray, his cheeks sunken, but his eyes shone with curiosity and interest.

The two of them set up camp and began separate journeys into their own and each other's pasts. That evening they sat close together in the circle around the campfire. They both beat drums and listened as Marvin and I gave our welcome talks that are designed to take the men down into their bodies.

Midway into Saturday, after a full morning of stories, sharing, and peeling pain away from our onionlike memories, we broke for lunch. Jim came up to Marvin and said, "I want to thank you guys for everything. It's been great for me and my dad. I've really gotten a lot out of it, but I've decided I got things to do back in town, so I'm going to boogie." "Are you sure that's what you need to do?" Marvin asked Jim as Jim hugged us both. "Yes," he said, and headed for his car. "What about your dad?" I asked. "Oh, he's going to stay. He's gotten a ride back with one of the men. He's loving this thing, but I really do have to get back to town and see my girlfriend. 'Bye—thanks."

Mr. Waitman had decided to come for his son. It wasn't time for Jim to go further. It was long past time for Mr. Waitman to feel what he felt and mourn the things that he'd lost—maybe even his son.

Mr. Waitman wept a lot during that weekend: Sixty-five and opening like a flower, shaking like a reed in the wind, and committed as any man present. Maybe the son will be back; maybe he won't. But Mr. Waitman will never be the same again and neither will we. His presence—and his willingness to stay—spoke to us all and left us changed and envious of a son who had a father who could not only come with him, but stay after he'd left. We honored him.

We honored another older man in Santa Fe. Mr. Brown was seventy years old. His son Luke was thirty and gay. At our gatherings most men are between thirty and forty-five and are usually heterosexual, though more and more gay men are involving themselves with those of us who respect individual, sexual lifestyles. Mr. Brown was straight, a Christian, very conservative, and a family man who loved his son enough to be at the gathering with him, letting his presence there say loudly to one hundred and thirty men and his son that he loved him, despite the fact he was gay. We were all touched by the gracefulness with which he related to all of

145

us. He went through all of the experiential exercises, camped on the ground in a tent, and got up each morning feeling no worse than the rest of us and looking a lot better than some. He drummed, he danced, and he wept. But mostly he smiled a knowing smile that must only come to those who go seven decades or longer and learn to accept life and its sons as they are.

He was the oldest to attend our gatherings so far. Each time I hugged him and thanked him for being there, I felt the arms of my grandfather reaching out of the grave and grabbing me close to his chest. While I honored Mr. Brown, I grieved my grandfather's death.

Mr. Percy had white hair that could make cotton turn green with envy. He was a scientist by profession, a seeker by disposition, and still healing at sixty-five. When the younger men paid tribute to the elders, as we always do, his voice cracked and his eyes shone, and it was plain that he was happy he came.

I was as glad as he was for his presence. When I lead the ceremony that recognizes the men over fifty, as Bly suggests, I always go deep into my own stuff, my own unfinished father business. I never go too far away from the role of facilitator, but I do let the moments move me closer to the spirit of my father as he lives in the present and the spirit of my grandfathers as they were in the past.

I ask the twenty or so men to sit in a place of honor and request that they speak to the group for as long as they wish. Most are usually so touched and overwhelmed that they only talk for a few minutes each. A few weep because they never, before that moment, considered themselves to be elders or to "know" enough to be honored for their years.

Some look confused because they still see themselves as "little boys" trying to deal with their dads. More than a few feel guilty and say so. "I don't deserve to be here," said Mr. Jackson. "I've done nothing special. I've hurt my children, disappointed my wife." He paused for a few moments. "But maybe I do after all. I have survived alcohol, sickness, two divorces, and a bankruptcy. Maybe I do belong here."

Each time I lead the honoring of the older men at these gatherings I think I won't be affected. The truth is, as soon as we call them up and they sit down, a lump sits right in the middle of my throat. These are the men who have reached fifty and older and are still willing to fight for their lives and grieve the decades of pain that after this long might easily be ignored or anesthetized. These men are still trying. I'm always touched by the fact that they come in part to listen to and work with me, like my father never did, and probably never will. And they always tell me they're "proud" of me, as my father never could do when I was a kid. And I get to be in the presence of older people, which is something I seldom do, living in a segregated society.

Mr. Percy, naked from the waist up, came over and we held each other after the ceremony. I touched his leathery, loose skin, looked into his wise eyes and cried, suddenly aware that we don't touch old people nearly enough, nor do we let them touch us. We don't see old men's bodies, so we don't know what to expect from our own as years transfigure them. We also don't get the benefit of their years of wisdom. Mr. Percy and I held each other—older man and man becoming older—and cried. Then we danced with delight. Later I asked him to sit by me; we held hands and exchanged glances that spoke of a kind of love all men long for—a kind of meaning that comes to our lives when the older rub shoulders with the younger. I'm thankful for these older men. I'm proud to touch them.

Sometimes I see the face of my aging father in theirs and I grieve. And in those same moments I celebrate these men's sobriety, success, and sanity. And I'm damned glad and honored to be a part of it all. Thank you, Mr. Percy from Little Rock. Thank you, all the men I respectfully and gladly call sir and mister.

After the honoring of the elders, the men gather in a clearing in a field where the grass comes up to their calves; they're anticipating an initiation ritual they've waited for their whole life.

It's Sunday afternoon, and it's cool in New Mexico. They are tired and seem slightly tense as Marvin makes the opening announcement that sets the stage for a ceremony they didn't know was coming but became quickly aware they'd missed when they were twelve or thirteen years old.

We draw a line on the ground that separates the men from their fathers, their childhoods, their mothers, their adolescence, and their forgetfulness. This line is made of sticks and stones and even rolled-up bandannas; it helps them to remember the manhood they've never honored.

Because most men have never been initiated into the world of men by older men, Marvin and I ask the men over fifty to cross the line first so that they can be on the other side to greet the younger ones. As they prepare to do so, a steady drumbeat is played by two drummers.

Mr. Perkins stands straight, his gray hair blowing in the breeze. He stands there and cries before crossing. He cries for the sixty-seven years it's taken him to do this. He then gently leans over into my and Marvin's arms, and sobs loudly. After a few moments, he steps over the line with pride and dignity, totally unencumbered by his culture, which never taught him the power of this ritual. He seems to move through mythic time, like some ancient warrior, wounded, but not dead; indeed, perhaps more alive than ever. Once across, he turns around smiling, prepared to greet the rest of his life as a welcomed male. He then turns to his younger brothers as they form two rows and make similar but unique journeys up to and across that line.

Watching the men come up to the ceremonial marker that separates their childhood chaos from a brotherhood of grief and gratefulness is to me the high point of the gathering.

These moments are full of drum sounds, wind, and wonder; they are eternal and primordial. The men are mourning the fact that they are thirty, forty-three, or fifty-seven and have never been blessed into the world of men by elders and brothers. The experience watching the younger men as they are whispered to, held, and welcomed by the men over fifty is simply indescribable.

The first time I led such a ritual, I was not truly touched until a gray-bearded man, who I highly respected because of his history and willingness to work on himself, held me and whispered the words, "I'm so proud of you. Welcome to the world of men." I started bawling. This man over fifty, my elder, had listened to me all weekend, had been to other lectures I'd given, read my books, and crawled inside my soul. He then said what I'd longed to hear from a father, a grandfather, an uncle, or some male in my immediate family who was sober and safe.

Now as the men move through the line of elders, they form a circle that surrounds those coming through, creating a masculine nest. The initiation—which is only one of many symbolic rites that must be performed and felt—slowly comes to its close. The circle is complete as I join them, my brothers in ritual, ceremony, and manhood. Several of the men talk about how touched they are and how much the arms of an elder meant. They say how much they value the smile of brothers who are there to support rather than compete, and who silently vow to cooperate and enter into a quiet collusion of their growth and healing.

I thank the men for letting me be a part of this weekend and I tell them how much I appreciate them listening to me, reading my books, and being with me on my journey to recover the masculinity I almost lost. I thank Marvin, and other partners not present, for putting together all the men's gatherings that I've been a part of, and I tell Marvin how much I appreciate him as a man.

There's more said by him and others, more feelings of joy expressed, along with a little sadness, as we come to the end of an event that will not soon be forgotten. I look into a sixteen-year-old boy's eyes and tear up with envy, sadness, and gratefulness. I look at the sky and think about all the times I just wanted to fly up into it and be carried away by the wind to some place other than where I was.

At these gatherings, I know that the earth is my home, and men are healing, and the sky is to be only visited and viewed from below. It's in these clearings that I am reminded in a very deep way that the men's movement is a part of Mother Earth, and that saving her and her children, and loving the women and men who want to love us is what the men's movement is about; it is also about forgiving those who couldn't love us the way we wanted to be loved. And finally it's about forgiving ourselves for all the big and little disasters that we've caused in our lives and in the lives of others. It's about finally shaking free of our addictions and codependency one day at a time and feeling each feeling as we become ready.

The circle breaks and the drumming and the dancing and laughing begins. Men dance with each other, laugh and cry, and some read poetry. Who would have thought it possible only a few years ago? Construction workers, lawyers, doctors, landscapers, accountants, all men united in ritual, ceremony, recovery, and sanity. If you could only see their faces.

It is possible that I'll be seeing your face at a men's gathering some day. Or if you're a woman reading this, hang on, we're healing and heading straight for your hearts while opening our own, and someday real soon we'll be doing a men and women's gathering. Then we'll dance together, drum together, hold each other, and tell each other our deepest truths. For we know ". . . the sexes are more related than we think, and the great renewal of the world will perhaps consist in this that men and women, freed of all false feelings and reluctances will seek each other not as opposites, but as brother and sister, as neighbors and will come together as human beings. . . ." (Rilke, *Letters to a Young Poet*)

# THE MASCULINE LOVER

## Opening to the Women in Our Lives

He hardly ever dreams about her anymore. He tells you that he loves the woman he's with and thinks she's great—best thing that ever happened to him. But you don't believe him, even though you may want to. Ask him how long it was after the separation, the breakup, the divorce before he met the new woman, and he'll tell you after a couple of weeks, a couple of months, a couple of drinks she was moving in or he was at least wishing she would.

Jessie knew he had never grieved the loss of his first wife. He knew that he should, he'd read enough to know that. Carolyn, his would-be wife, knew it as well. If you walked up to Carolyn and asked her, "Has Jessie grieved his last love to completion?" she might say she didn't know. But she does know. She feels it when she least expects to. Perhaps when they're making love, he looks away at just the wrong moment and loses himself in memory for what is to him only seconds, but to her is an eternity. It's not usually anything as obvious as him calling her by his old lover's name, although that's happened on occasion. But she frequently sees his ex-lover's ghost gliding around him as he gestures to Carolyn to come to him. She knows that sometimes he wants her to make the memory of his last lover go away or at least to soothe the pain.

Most importantly, he knows that he hasn't grieved his loss—his old love, and maybe even more than one old love. But he's afraid. The unresolved grief is a tiny string that strangles both him and his new lover—indeed all of them—man, present lover, and ex-lover. For the ex-lover can feel him holding on to her even though she may be miles away. She feels the tug as he tries to pull her back into the present for fear of a future without her. If he grieves, he's afraid she'll finally disappear and he will be back as she first found him; slightly open, vulnerable, and ready to love and be loved. When his old lover left, it hurt so much that he held onto her with all the strength his psyche could muster. That way no one would ever touch him like that again. No one would get that close. No one would ever hurt him again.

Or he may want to let her go. He may want to grieve. He may love the woman he's with. But he's also afraid that if he grieves the long-ago love that his present love will not understand and may leave him—and where would he be then? No ex-love, no present love—twice the pain—twice left.

What he doesn't know is what I didn't know for a long time. If we don't grieve that last one, the next one knows it and will probably have to leave. She can't get into the spot on the left side of our chest where we hide ourselves from her and can't let her in. If we don't grieve, we can't go on, but we can go on with our lives *while* we grieve. Usually we even will be supported in the process, as long as we're honest about it and communicate about what we're doing and why.

If I tell a woman, "I'm still grieving my last love, and I've done enough to want to be with you still, but I need time to feel," she'll respect me. And she'll know that it is likely that some day she might be loved so deeply as to be honored with sincere grief should she have to go.

What I didn't know was that grieving Phyllis and Deborah and Karen, the loves of my youth, did not make them disappear off the planet or make them leave my soul. Rather, grieving them allowed me to let them go and let the good of each of them become a part of me that I cherish more than I can say. Many of the things that attracted me to them have, with time, shown up in my own character.

The lost lovers leave us emptier of their presence than grieving does. Grieving opens us to the person we presently are. Then we don't cling to our new lover so tightly, for we know our own strength. But we can love her. And she will have the opportunity to love a man, not a ghost.


## LETTING GO OF A LOST LOVE

The lover leaves. What is left is a hole, a shell, a wound, a grief that streams out of the man's pores. Every wound, every abandonment, every unshed tear comes rushing out to be remembered, observed, felt, experienced, expressed, and released. The man who refuses to descend into his soul and examine his woundedness at times like these, moves into self-pity, denial, and self-destruction. He'll get up in the morning and leave his face unwashed, his hair uncombed, and his stomach unfed. Or he'll work seventy hours a week to numb the hole made by her departure. Some will go to a bar every night, and instead of putting a quarter into a telephone and calling a friend for support, the quarter gets dropped into a jukebox to play songs that tell him he's nothing now that she's gone.

He'll play games of denial with his body and mind. The body will ache for her, and the her before, and the her before that, all the way back to high school, and even further back to missing his mom and father who abandoned him. The mind will say, "To hell with her. I didn't love her anyway. There are more fish in the sea. Good riddance." But at night, if the body has not been completely anesthetized during the day, he will cry out. The body will betray the mind and run a sneak play and say, "You really did love her. You really have got to get your shit together, or you're going to lose another, and another, and another!"

The mind filled with propaganda and programming, silences the body's aches and yearnings for healing by prematurely seeking out another would-be lover to remove the last from his memory, his blood, and bones. And so the man, unable to grieve, will have "soul mate" number twenty-six move in before the last woman's love, luggage, and furniture are completely out of his sight or house. The new woman moves in before the divorce papers are signed, before the grief is observed, before the man stops dreaming of the last woman, and destroying himself in the present. His new love will see that his last love was not important enough to be grieved, even though perhaps he had been with her for fourteen years and had two children. She will always doubt his depth and his ability really to love her. He will tire himself with his self-pity, and others will soon tire of him as well. He'll need too much attention from them.

True grieving is empowering, energizing, and ennobling. The loss of a lover, parent, child, job, or close friend can be a fact of life, and a fact the body must live through and respond to. How much grief-work he has done determines how much he'll have to do after each loss that life leaves him with. If the loss of childhood has been grieved, then when a man's child grows up and leaves for kindergarten or college, the grief will be less than if he hasn't. If the college "love of his life" has been gone for two decades, but the grief hasn't been dealt with, then when the present lover leaves, they'll both merge to be grieved and released.

Most men and women have not witnessed grieving done in a healthy way. Although we have seen a lot of self-pity in its varied forms, most of us don't know how to grieve. We feel if it's anything like self-pity (which it isn't) we would rather avoid it. Thus the very state we're trying never to find ourselves in ends up being the same state we're in again and again.

Here's what real grief-work looks like. Your father dies, or your wife leaves: You get up everyday and you weep until your body doesn't want to anymore. You shower and shave, and even though you're dripping wet when the anger surfaces, you grab a tennis racket and beat your bed until the water dries, and you're wet with your own sweat and you take another shower. You make yourself the healthiest breakfast you can, and eat it even if you don't want to. Before you go to work or school, you write a letter or journal about your feelings. You feel every one of those feelings down to the bone. And when you go to work, if you can't take time off, you don't let anyone there tell you: "Get back in the saddle." "Pull yourself up by the bootstraps." "Let's go out for some beers after work." "Cheer up." "It can't be that bad."

Instead, you find one or two people who love you, who themselves know grief and choose it over self-pity, and tell your story of hurt and loneliness; for the father you never had, or the love you forgot to feel or give, or the times you forgot to forgive or ask forgiveness. You ask them to play racketball with you, or take a walk, or go to a movie. You know that one or two will not be able to be there at all times, so you find a support group, a men's group, or a Twelve-Step meeting and listen carefully to the experience, strength, and hope you find in each one. Maybe you'll want or need to find a therapist to add to your growing ability to ask for support. If you do, I hope you'll make sure they will not turn off your grief due to their fear of their own, or their misguided belief that grief should be medicated away, lest it turn into depression. Self-pity turns into depression and disease. Grieving frees up the body, the soul, and the mind, and keeps our center emptied out and allows love and joy to come in its place.

The better a man takes care of himself during these difficult times, the sooner he passes through the dark night. The more damage and denial he does to himself, the longer he will take to heal, and the deeper will be the mistakes he makes along the way. More hearts will be broken in his attempt to heal his broken heart. When a man grieves, he walks through the "valley of the shadow of death," but he doesn't have to do this alone. When he comes out on the other side, he'll be lighter, less intense, less addicted, and

157

ready to love and be loved. If a lover comes near, he'll be ready for intimacy, and if she doesn't, he'll still be all right because he can now take care of himself. He has a support group of people in his life whom hopefully he'll keep and nurture and be nurtured by even with a new love.

## BECOMING THE MASCULINE LOVER

The man who can't grieve, can't say much that comes from his heart or gut. He talks from his head most of the time, if he talks at all. He'll tell you what he wants, what he should have, but say damn little about what he needs.

I remember four years ago sitting in my hotel room in Santa Fe, talking long distance to soul mate number twenty-two. After an hour's worth of my focusing on her, she finally paused and said, "We've been talking for over an hour now about what I need. What do you need?" My mouth fell open, silence descended on it, my tongue was frozen. Finally my facial muscles moved, and I simply uttered, "What do I need? I'll have to get back to you later. I don't know what I need." And I didn't. At that moment it seemed like my whole life revolved around me figuring out what other people needed and how I could provide it. I can honestly say I couldn't recall having ever been asked or asking myself what I needed. And it's such a basic question.

Men who feel can be with women as they feel. And while I can't claim that I feel my own feelings even seventy-five percent of the time, I'm getting better at it. When a man gets better, a relationship changes in a variety of ways. If his partner is working on herself as well, then boundaries are drawn, enforced, and respected. For example: "When you're angry, I do not want to be called names. When you're going through stuff with your father, I need you not to dump it on me."

As more and more men open up to the women they love, they will stop using the relationship to recover what has been lost or heal what has been wounded. When I am angry or sad about my relationship, and it feels overwhelming or highly charged and I can't contain it, I have a number of choices. I can take these feelings first to either another man, or a Twelve-Step meeting, or a therapist. I may work it through by journaling, or discharge it in some way physically through exercise in the woods. I ask that my partner do the same.

When a man moves closer to his own masculinity, he lets his "yes" mean yes, and his "no" mean no. Before I did a lot of my own work, "no" wasn't in my vocabulary except as I'd use it on myself by telling myself "no." "You don't need rest . . ." or "No, you don't deserve a good relationship." I basically couldn't tell other people no. Especially women. So my "yes" didn't really mean much because it didn't really come out of choice, but rather from fear. I was afraid to tell people no because they might not think well of me, or they may be disappointed in my performance.

The masculine lover doesn't (except on bad days) dump his woundedness on a woman and expect her to heal him. He doesn't let women or men dump their woundedness on him. He's firm in his resolve, yet flexible when the situation warrants, but most importantly, he doesn't compromise his recovery for anyone, any amount of sex, money, power, or out of fear.

The masculine lover says: "After decades of constant

compromise of my essential self, I will not do so to be loved by you. I'll compromise on where we live, where we eat, how many children we have, what movie we see, where our children will go to school, but not on matters that jeopardize my soul—I need you to stop drinking in this house. I need the abuse to stop. I demand safety. I need to be nurtured. I need love. I need to express my anger. I need you to express yours. I need mutual respect and equality. I will not settle for less than what I know I deserve, which is health. I will not compromise my recovery to be in a relationship."

The walls erected by woundedness come down one brick at a time, and are slowly replaced by boundaries. The wounded lover hides behind these walls and you can't see him. You can see one who firmly stands on the other side of a boundary. It's usually a man who loves very much and is going to stay with you for as long as it is right and healthy to do so. But he may not do what you want him to, or be like you want him to be, or feel the way you feel. The masculine lover has his feminine with him, his inner child, his wise, older man, and thus he's not going to be responsible for his lover's feelings, or try to fix her. And he may slip into old patterns on days that he's too tired, or hungry, or stressed. But he'll see them quickly and make a call for support. Each time he does, he'll reduce the time it takes to get back to his new self.

His lover will be able to feel her feelings if she can, and he won't be intimidated by them, and thus won't need to shut them off. He'll listen, seldom interrupt. And when he needs to speak, he will speak more and more often words of empathy and understanding. He'll cry when he needs to, even if he just cried yesterday. He'll get angry and do so appropriately. He'll be close to other men and allow them to support him. He won't be a perfect partner, but he will be perfectly content to partner as he chooses, rather than letting some pattern push him into and out of a relationship before he's ready.

The man who can grieve and feel is the same man who can be playful, spontaneous, curious, risk-taking within a committed relationship, as well as outside one. He'll be fun to be with and he'll finally feel safe enough to be all he can be. He will support his lover in doing the same. Each man will vary in all that has been said and demonstrate positive masculinity in a number of ways that don't appear in this book. Every man will find a way to be his own man.

## FREEDOM TO BECOME

The men's gathering was to be held in a place my ex-girlfriend Laurel and I visited nine years ago to that very month. It was then and is now a beautiful spot, a small retreat center outside Las Vegas, New Mexico. This weekend would undoubtedly be a painful walk into the past.

Nine years before the publication of *The Flying Boy*, before I joined men's groups and held weekend retreats, and before the years of my own therapy and recovery work, Laurel and I walked and gazed into the faces of the mountains that multiplied meaning and purpose just by looking at them. She and I passed the first evening in a hot tub under stars that were so close I had to turn away from them. I was drinking wine so fast and furiously that each gulp banished true intimacy.

The next day, lying in the middle of a carpeted room that

looked out over a New Mexico paradise, Laurel tried to give me a massage. Her hands were tender as she rubbed in the scented oil along with her love. But I wasn't there to feel and receive. Having learned to numb my body since early childhood and having never in my then thirty years received a massage, I was frozen with fear. And I soon stopped the entire process. Just as I couldn't let other women in when they tried to hold me or make love to me, I couldn't let her in when she simply touched me.

Standing at the center of the circle of men, surrounded by the same mountains seen by the same silent stars, I was just as numb as I was back then—the difference being only that I knew I was numb. The poignancy of my being there was too great, too overwhelming.

I stood before one hundred and thirty men who were ready to speak about their pain, and I was too afraid to let my own surface. I wanted to believe that the years and the meetings and the men's groups and the therapy had made the pain disappear. And yet there I was nine years later still trying to feel.

I looked into the faces of the men and said, "If we could only let in what surrounds us now—the sky, the mountains, this valley, the love—we'd be mostly healed, having already done what we came here to do. If I could only let this and you in." A tear came and I couldn't continue—my tears and pain were instantly swallowed, clogging my throat. I thought to myself, "Perhaps I should just gracefully bow out and let my buddies and cofacilitators do this weekend while I try to get in touch with the pain I still try to bury from time to time."

The next day it rained, and we gathered in an old barn that smelled of hay and transported us back to simpler times, to a grandfather or uncle, or maybe a father. I couldn't hold in the grief any longer. I started a talk about grieving the lovers, the wives, the girlfriends of our past. I told the story of how all weekend I'd been choking down the memories, sidestepping the mental pictures of a woman I knew almost a decade before, a woman who would never know how much I had changed, how much I hadn't. She couldn't know how much I was afraid to be massaged, to be sober, to be intimate, to be close.

I closed the talk with the men and myself in tears. I got up and walked down to the house that held the memories and placed myself in the middle of that carpeted floor and cried like it was yesterday that I lost her.

The rest of the weekend I was fully there, fully in touch with my feelings, and full of grief and, at the same time, full of happiness, knowing I was healing. I became even more convinced that memory and the body and our grief are not regulated by the clock, the calendar, or the brain. Grief comes and goes when it's ready.

Only after I let the sadness out could I see that I'd come full circle. I was at peace and could see that if a massage was ever offered again, with love as its only price and reward, that I'd receive it.

And two months later, in a log cabin in Vancouver with mountains watching, right after a sober soak in a hot tub, a woman I love moved her hands across my chest and back. These tender hands were warm and loving. And they were felt and appreciated; the process was not prematurely halted out of fear, but fully taken in. And the process of recovery deepened as my love of self and her multiplied.

# PART FOUR

# THE FUTURE

# THE NEW PARADIGM

## The New Male

T he men's movement is creating a new model of true masculinity. This new paradigm will be built upon the rock-solid foundation of cooperation. The old sense of competition must die. And the men who hold themselves out as leaders of the men's movement must be the first to show the way out of the sickness competition has created in the hearts and souls of men for thousands of years. These "leaders" must answer the challenge and move over and stand shoulder to shoulder as brothers in a new era, rather than as bosses, captains, generals, and masters or gurus.

Men in this movement toward health and wholeness must and will demand that they have an equal say and role in all phases of their own growth and the healing of their planet. The "leaders" must do their own soul-work to discover how they came to feel and believe that there's "not enough" to go around, and thus horde or lay claim to information as if it's property, and not provide direct support for other men to claim their full power and share in their ability to lead. We must feel how and why we need to always have to produce, perform, and win at any cost.

If we fail to shift from the old paradigm to the new masculinity, it will be because of men who continue to compete instead of lead: How many books did I write? How many came to my workshops or gatherings? Who has been on TV or in magazines more often? The old "Them" versus "Us" war, which generates factions and schisms and blind loyalty, blinds men to the fact that there is plenty of everything to go around, plenty of different points of view, plenty of different kinds of wounds and needs.

Jack Knight, a therapist I know, provides a good example of this sense of cooperation. When he started his private practice, after having done a lot of work on himself, he put behind him a lot of his fears and his father's programming. He put the client's well-being before his own pocketbook and ego. Even when he first opened his practice and only had a few clients (specializing in men's issues was not done then since so few men went into therapy, and if they did, most didn't stay long enough for it to pay off), he would work with them until he felt they could benefit more from a body therapy such as Rolfing, or more specialized dance or movement therapy, such as Feldenkrais, or a Twelve-Step program. He'd make it clear to his clients he'd be glad to see them while they were doing these other necessary and timely healing activities, but if they couldn't afford both, he'd see them once a month to help them integrate what they were doing, and be an anchor while they went through their process. Some therapists thought he was on the fast track to failure—first for specializing in men; second for supporting them to go to other counselors or therapists. Jack even caught himself considering the sanity of it all from time to time. The clients, however, saw Jack as the compassionate man he was, and as an extremely caring counselor they could gladly refer their friends to. "He really cares more about our health than money," was the feeling they had. Every time he'd put them first, they'd send him three or four referrals. He became so successful and proved to all of the hurt adult children from dysfunctional families, where scarcity was the norm, that there really is enough to go around.

Another example is a personal one. In April of 1991, I agreed to have my work featured in a special four-part series on the men's movement for PBS. I was high with delight. I then thought about it for a few days and became troubled. I called the producer back and said, "I'd love to do it, but only if I can invite men who are breaking new ground with me to be on the show. I need to be a part of a team more than I need to have my ego fanned." He agreed and was delighted. The new paradigm is beginning to appear in my new psyche.

Just the other day, I got invited to do a workshop at the Omega Institute in New York. I accepted, then called back and said I'd like to bring a friend and a partner in the journey. Jed Diamond, a major voice in the men's movement, will be my guest. Jed called the other day and said, "I'm going to do a workshop at Esalen and would like for you to join me."

Yes, we have egos—big ones—they eat a lot of energy and attention, but some of us have a greater need to be supported, share, and heal together, and come in out of the cold and drop the lone-wolf, "Marlboro man" routine many of us perform because we're scared. We want to serve, see, and be seen as equals, not employees, bosses, stars, or second bananas.

The new masculinity is inclusive, not exclusive; embracing the differences, not embarrassing those who see things differently. And most important, I believe it's supportive. The men who are out front speaking and writing and leading workshops must not give in to backbiting, criticizing, and categorizing. I believe we must support men on all levels— grass roots to international—to come out and lead with us. We, as men, must feel the fear our fathers gave us and move through it. Our fathers said we can't trust anybody, so we must learn to trust each other, lead and follow each other. When it's our turn to speak, we do so because we have something to say and share, and because we have listened and heard. Yes, there may be chiefs, but they "serve" based on their willingness to be supported and they sit in a circle shoulder to shoulder. And when their season is over, they sit again, shoulder to shoulder to learn from the rest.

Finally, the new masculinity will make more room for failing and show that it's not the same thing as being a failure. A healthy regard and respect for trying and failing will be demonstrated.

Our fathers couldn't feel their fears and move through them, because they didn't have support from other men to do so. They said things like, "Nothing ventured, nothing gained," but when it came time for "following their bliss," they were so afraid to fail and not be able to pay their bills on time, that they sucked on a bottle, sucked the life out of their jobs, wives, or children to make them forget their real failing was in not trying. They turned their unfelt fear into anger, and stuffed it until it either became rage or stone-cold silence. And they passed on these stuck feelings to their sons.

They didn't show or tell us that failing is what leads ultimately to success. When Dan Jones and I train therapists in our theories and techniques of emotional release-work, we notice how their fear of failing makes them afraid to take risks. They watch as we work with someone. We try maybe six or eight different things before one works, and the participant releases deep emotion. The observers tend to focus on the one thing that worked, forgetting the failed attempts, and thus not seeing that each risked and failed try was an important and necessary step that led to the one that worked.

Once men embrace their own failings they can love those who frequently fail due to their humanness. If we had had fathers who had said, "Son, no matter what you do, or how successful you become, I'll love you, I'll be there for you. And I'll share with you the areas I failed in," the son would see in action and feel in his body that failing is a part of success.

The new masculinity will greet failing as their fathers could not do, and then our sons and daughters will not feel ashamed when they don't always succeed, win, and triumph. And they won't be driven to succeed at the high cost of their health, trying to show their parents how it's done, or to let their parents vicariously live out their unrealized dreams.

## GROUPS AND GATHERINGS

I often get asked to describe my approach to men's groups and gatherings, but I'm not suggesting that anyone else hold men's groups in this manner. I hope this brief, general description will be useful to men looking to establish their own groups, methods, and voices.

Dan Jones and I have been partners in facilitating men's groups and as cotherapists for adult children's groups for years. Marvin Allen and I have done several men's gatherings. Before that I'd been a loner all my life. I had lectured and taught at universities by myself and still enjoy lecturing and doing day-long workshops alone, and of course, writing is a very lonely endeavor. But when it comes to working with men, it's just more practical and enjoyable to buddy-up with a partner. Two men, shoulder to shoulder, back to back, can see more, hear more, be more. And while there is no such thing as perfect partners, I and the men I work with have a deep, growing relationship that each passing year enhances.

In groups and the gatherings, safety is the most important ingredient. In a safe environment feelings can be experienced and expressed. Participants can receive tremendous amounts of support from us coleaders and the other men in the groups.

Men's groups and gatherings are physical as well as psychological and spiritual. Dan and I work with ten to twelve men in a group for two-hour sessions. About four to six men in that group get to "work" on some issue or concern. The work is really about helping the men feel their bodies, their feelings, their pasts, their patterns, and, through experiential processes and support, break out of the destructive behavior that binds and cripples them. The other men in the group vicariously experience what a particular man is working on, and if it restimulates something in them, they will have a turn to "work" next, rather than confronting the man working or interrupting. In other words, the groups and the gatherings are supportive and not confrontational. We believe we engage in enough confrontation in our daily lives to last a lifetime. Indeed, many of our childhoods were one big war waged between us and some unsupportive person.

Our groups and gatherings are about feeling and discharging the emotions we've been stuffing. They are also about cognitive restructuring and reframing, and forgiving and grieving and laughing and sharing the deepest part of ourselves in the company of men who are willing to be there for us as we are for them.

I try to cofacilitate my groups and gatherings by being a brother rather than a therapist—a fellow traveler who has some skills and information that might be useful. In other words, if my own feelings emerge in a group or gathering, they get dealt with right there, if it's appropriate.

In the groups and gatherings, men work hard on the following issues: the father-son wound, and their relationship to their mothers, women, other men, children, and bosses. They struggle over their fears about money, death, sex, retirement, dependency, and depression. They mourn lost childhoods, lack of contact with and caring for their inner child and the aging of their bodies. They find their feminine sides, their "Wildmen," their bodies, and their joy. They learn to trust other men, themselves, and the women in their lives. They allow love to come in. And they are helped to become whole.

There is so much more than I can communicate here that goes on in men's gatherings, men's groups, men's minds, and men's bodies. What I've offered is only one-one-hundredth of the emotion, energy, trust, fear, courage, hurt, and joy that is present or lying dormant waiting to be released. And I must reiterate that a men's group or gathering doesn't "mend" the wounds. The mending is done by the men, alone or with each other, over time. The gatherings, conferences, and groups are just catalysts that speed and deepen the healing.

At some point you'll stand up, maybe at dinner or wake up one more time at 2:00 A.M., and you'll decide from someplace deep in your soul that it's time. Time to do the work we wish we didn't have to do.

Some men's groups are led by competent men who are doing their own work, some by men who ride fads like wild horses blindly going over cliffs. You'll know. You'll feel it in your gut. You'll quickly sense whether or not these groups or gatherings are just macho bullshit, run like marine boot camps. If a group or gathering demeans, diminishes, shames, or hurts—get out. Seek a place and a person who by their very being says, "I'm safe. This place is safe. No shaming here."

There are men who have long been on the scene, and others are just appearing, to help guide their brothers into not so well-lit places. Robert Bly is one, along with James Hillman, Shepherd Bliss, Michael Meade, and John Stokes. These men represent what is being called the Mythopoetic Men's Movement. The emphasis in this part of the movement is on myth, story, fairy tale, and poetry as the main tools, mixed with Jungian psychology, drumming, mask-making, and other rituals and ceremonies. Jed Diamond, Marvin Allen, and I, and others are coming from a recovery and therapeutic background, and yet still emphasize and value the mythopoetic.

Another major part of the men's movement has been led

since the early seventies by people such as Warren Farrell, Herb Goldberg, and others who have been doing men's work with a feminist slant. Then there are a number of men working with gay men's issues, and fathers for equal time and rights with their children. There are good men too numerous to mention in all these parts of the men's movement. All deserve a salute for the good work they're doing.

The men's movement is an umbrella that many are under and many more are looking for. The essential thing for me is that the umbrella remains large enough to shelter and that we support each other and that we continue to bring in others of different races and socioeconomic backgrounds.

While we work under this gigantic parasol, we must dialogue and communicate our fears and feelings as we receive the fallout, the fear, and the hailstones of anger and misunderstanding that are bound to fall on us from time to time.

Many men come to groups and gatherings and then leave to go back to small towns—or large ones—where they can't find a men's group. The solution: Start one yourself. Look inside and see what you love, what you want, what you have to share. Perhaps you can find one other man, then later two more and then maybe four other men to get together with once a week to tell each other your dreams. Or perhaps you like poetry, so you find others to read and discuss how poems make your body hunger, hurt, and heal. Or you might start a men's Twelve-Step group. The important elements must be a shared commitment to be there regularly, to share, to listen, and to honor the feelings and issues that come up in a safe, nurturing environment. You don't have to have a therapist to be in the men's movement. You just need to be a man who yearns for more men in your life and desires more healing in your relationships with others and the planet.

## AFFIRMATION AND ACTION AGAINST FAILURE

Earlier, I spoke about men and failing and said it was different from failure. The men's movement can be a failure if it doesn't accomplish some moral imperatives, but gets side-tracked into becoming just another men's club.

If the men's movement only reaches the white middle-class male, due to unconsciously or consciously imposed exclusivity, it will be a failure. The white men who are reached will be helped in the short term, but if the ideas, information, and feelings are not crossing color lines drawn by our forefathers, then all men and women will end up paying a heavy toll. We must make ourselves and our information available to any men who are willing to use it.

Five black men were sitting in a sea of white. Midway through the workshop, I approached one of these men, whose name was Burt, and asked him, "How did you come to be here?" He knew before I told him why I was asking. He knew that black men and other men of color seldom come to a gathering such as this one in Sacramento. He knew because he, too, seldom saw anyone with skin as dark as his own at such meetings. This lack of color hurt him as much—no, more, much more—than it did me. I've known for some time that the men's movement and its sibling, the recovery movement, have not yet swept through the hearts, minds, and homes of most black people. While a few Mexican-American men have been bringing their experiences to such gatherings, it's been very difficult to bring in the community of minority men for hugging, healing, holding, Twelve-Step work, and drumming.

I've felt for quite a while that if the men's movement ends up drawing only the white middles and uppers, we will have failed. It won't diminish the work these men do on themselves and the healing that will occur, but it will feel very incomplete to me and many others, and ultimately the culture as a whole. It's my belief that all men need an opportunity to heal with other men. I know it's a romantic notion, but it's just such notions that sometimes balance the hard realist's point of view.

Suffice it to say that men of color are welcome and that while those of us who are white can't claim to know a black man's experience, we are willing to listen and learn.

This is what I learned when Burt answered my question: "Some white men know they have problems. Some white men don't. Black men are taught that they don't have problems." He paused and looked at his four friends and then back at me. "Black men don't have problems. We have been told our whole life We Are The Problem."

His words shot into my chest and exited through my back like a bullet. I thanked him and his friends for caring enough to be at my workshop and for sharing their insights. I was stunned by their honesty.

While I don't have the details, I know that Robert Bly and James Hillman have made a commitment to men of color by providing training to those interested in working within their communities.

We at the Austin Men's Center are setting up training programs for men of color to help them learn how to work with men more effectively and set up men's support groups that address their own unique issues, while incorporating the principles and tools of the men's movement. It's time to reach out and cross racial ditches dug by ancestors who were blinded by ignorance, greed, racism, and poverty. It's past time.

Other possible pitfalls to be avoided: If the men's movement pushes to become political and ideological, rather than spiritual and emotional first, it will not bear fruit, instead it will wither on the vine. If it establishes a strong spiritual and emotional base, there will be massive political implications. But if its "leaders" promote factionalism, separatism, or single out one issue as the only cause men should fight for, and say their way to fight is the only way, then it will be doomed to disappear much like the fad, pop psychologies of the sixties and seventies.

If the men's movement does not embrace women and the women's movement (where it is spiritual and emotional), and cocreate a new dialogue, then it will be a failure.

While men must take time and create a sacred, safe space away from the company of women, we must learn to be and feel safe enough (in our own time) to cocreate safety and a sacred space in women's presence.

Picture this: A grove sits on the top of a hill in West Texas. The land rises up to meet the men who stand ready to protect it. They are surrounded by live oaks, mesquite, and wind. They drum and they dance, and cry out in pain and ecstasy. Not too far in the distance can be heard a different drumming and a deep kind of weeping. The women stand in their grove of trees, working on healing themselves while appreciating the men who are doing the same. Their drum sounds pulse through each body—sound, earth, and sky link man with woman—grief to grief, wound to wound.

Then there's a third grove where men and women sit next

to each other and hold each other, listening to and laughing with, and loving each other. Most of the projections onto the opposite sex are reclaimed. The mothers and fathers we should have had but didn't, have been released by feeling every feeling that came up. From each grove the men—the women—feeling equal, walk back to their towns, cities, work, routines, friends, and families. They're different: They stand taller and straighter, and their eyes are clearer for the tears they've cried. Their ears are more open because of the screams they let out and heard. Their bodies are felt, and are more connected to their minds than before. Soul and spirit, body and mind, man and woman united—not always—just a lot more often than before going into the groves to recover missing parts of themselves.

## EXERCISES FOR LETTING DAD GO

If you feel like doing the following exercises, I'll ask you to begin by taking a deep breath, finding a comfortable position, loosening anything that's tight or binding. This is about finding the father, feeling the father, and letting go of the feelings, and letting him go as well. You will only go as far and as deep as you're ready and you can stop at any time you wish and do more later. These exercises are a process and will not produce a final event. They will change you and your relationship to your father whether he's alive or dead.

*Exercise One:* Close your eyes and begin taking full deep breaths, letting your attention sink out of your head and down into your body. Breathing, feeling the tightness in your jaws and neck, letting your attention go down into your shoulders and chest. Taking a full deep breath, let your attention come out of your head and down into your stomach and back, breathing, feeling the tightness in your lower back (where lots of anger at Dad is carried). Taking full deep breaths, letting your attention come out of your head and blowing it to move through your genitals and buttocks and down through your legs and feet. Taking full deep breaths repeat the word "Father." Let the images come and the feelings come up. Taking a deep breath, see him, smell him, hear him. Remember how he dressed, how he sounded, letting the feelings come up as you let your attention go down to meet them. Feel whatever comes up. Let out any sound or tears that want out. Keep breathing, then when you're ready, repeat four times the word "Dad." Let any feelings come up as you repeat very slowly, "Dad, Dad . . ." Taking full deep breaths, see him, hear him, feel him. Then take another full deep breath and repeat the word "Daddy." Let the feelings that have been in your body come up as you try to keep your attention out of your head, moving it down into your body, feeling where Father, Dad, or Daddy rests. Then add to each as you breathe the words "my father," repeating it four times, feeling then "my dad," and finally "my daddy." Breathing and feeling, make sure you let out the sounds and sighs and tears.

After doing the exercise, you may want to write down what you felt. What parts of your body carries Father, Dad, or Daddy? Also note this exercise is twice as effective if done with others present and it is an exercise that can be done as many times as you feel it is useful to do.

\* \* \*

*Exercise Two:* It is best to do this exercise with another man who is willing to not only support you but willing to work himself, and it's also best to do it shortly after the last exercise.

Two men seat themselves comfortably in front of the other, letting the older man go first. Both men begin taking deep breaths, letting the attention go out of their heads and down into their bodies. After several breaths the younger man will hold out his hands and the older man, with eyes closed, will take his hands, but the hands he'll take will be his father's hands. The younger man will just breathe full deep breaths. The older man is to feel his father. See him, hear him, smell him. Remember him. Letting whatever feelings that want to come up, come up. Letting the sounds and sighs and tears out. Breathing, saying the following words to him as he see him in his mind's eye, "Good-bye, Dad, I've got to let you go." When he's ready, he drops the younger man's hands. The feeling that he doesn't want to let go may be the predominant one as, like most men, he may not feel like he's ever really had him and letting go is too difficult. Becoming aware of this difficulty, he adds the phrase, "Dad, I'm getting ready to let you go. I know I never had you, but I've got to let you go." He feels all of his feelings: anger, sadness, joy, whatever comes up, and then still feeling his feelings, he lets the younger partner have his turn. When both are finished, they talk about how they feel and give each other some appreciation for the good work they did—and give each other a hug.

A note on these exercises: Both are about letting Dad go, but they're really designed to let the negative, not-good-enough, abandoning, disappearing father go. These exercises are about you letting this father go so you can begin fathering yourself in healthier ways than he sometimes did for you when you were a child. You'll be especially pleased to know that there is no exercise that's ever been designed that will take out or cause you to let go of all the good things your father may have done, done for you, or taught you. These will always stay and heal you and increase your ability to refather yourself and be a better parent to your children and more adult and receptive and nurturing to your lover or wife.

## A NOTE ON PATIENCE

"Practice makes perfect," they said. It doesn't. They were wrong, just like they were wrong when they said, "Big boys don't cry." But practice and patience are the key points in a man's healing journey toward his masculinity. They are necessary elements in becoming the father to ourselves that we never had.

If a man thinks he *should* know how to express his feelings well after only a few weeks or months, then he is still holding onto his father. If a man practices expressing his feelings with friends, support groups, and those he loves, but fails from time to time, and tells himself it's okay, he'll get there. Keep trying. Remember: "I love you just as you are. You don't always have to do it right." He'll become a man who's safe for the little boy inside him and the little person inside all people. He'll become a good father to himself and will be a great dad to his own kids if he chooses to have children.

Patience. I wouldn't pray for it if I were you. But I sure

support you to cultivate it whenever you can. It makes the journey easier. Tom worked on his anger toward his father for several months in group. He got to it. He let it out. He really developed a healthy manner of releasing pent-up anger around or about nearly everything that angered him—both past and present. However, he couldn't cry. He hadn't cried in over twenty-eight years. The last time this small-framed, brown-eyed carpenter had cried was when he was ten and his dog died. His father bought him a new one the same day and told his son, "There's no need to cry any-more." I think he believed him or was shamed by him to the extent that he never cried again. When he told the story (which is one of the keys to healing; telling our story over and over until we feel it, and then can heal it) several of the men in the group wept. He got mad at once. "See, others can cry over my life, and their own. Why can't I, damn it?"

Tom came in for a private consultation with me. The tears didn't come during that hour either, but a feeling and a thought did. "Tom, I'd like for you to try something if you'd like. It will take some patience, and you'll have to practice it every day. I'd like for you to say the following phrase to yourself every morning and every evening before retiring; 'The tears will come when it's time.'"

He looked at me in disbelief. "That's all there is to it?" he asked. "You just want me to say, 'The tears will come when it's time'?"

"That's it. Every day and every night," I said. He left probably thinking, "Boy, I'm glad that was a free consulta-tion."

Eight weeks later my phone rang. I picked it up, and all

I could hear from the other end was deep sobbing. I just listened, not knowing who or what was going on. Finally after about three minutes I said, "Who is this?" Through the sniffing and sobbing the voice said, "The tears came. It's time."

Until a man can accept himself exactly where he is, and love himself exactly as he is, he can't get to where he wants or thinks he "ought" to be. If you can't remember anything else of what's been said, I hope you'll remember this. It's my belief that there is a power greater than ourselves that is in charge of our journey. Even though we always have choices, if we still believe we're "In Control" we've missed the point, the work, and probably our masculinity and recovery. That power, or presence, or higher self that guides us, combined with our willingness to show up and be patient with ourselves, will provide the right group, gathering, therapist, book, sponsor, teacher, time-off, lover, and healing when we're ready.

The tears will come when it's time, and so will the laughter, the joy, and the love you so rightly deserve. And when we engage ourselves, we'll be more fully able to love each other, and the people who love us, and perhaps have loved us all along.

I hope this book has helped men on their journey toward discovering and recovering their masculinity, while healing some old buried wounds. I hope it helped some women understand some of the men they know or have known. But more importantly, I hope it has helped people feel what it is to be a man, and how it hurts, and how they can heal.

I hope you'll go slow. Take care of yourself. Push aside your father's bones and fill that empty space he left with yourself, love, gentleness, and then give it back to the people you love. I hope you feel all your feelings, and know that none of them are negative or destructive unless they're not felt. Then I hope you forgive—your father, and yourself. But if you can't right now, or don't think you'll ever be able to, I hope you'll accept those feelings as well. I wish for you the best on your journey.


## AT OUR OWN WEDDINGS

One of the men stands by the huge fire. I don't know his name. He built the fire out of instinct, desire, and need. He gazes into it for hours, poking and prodding it to relieve himself of the tension that's been building in him for decades. He built the fire to satisfy some longing in him he can't even name; to warm something in him that's been frozen forever it seems. His eyes are glassy mirrors, reflecting the dance of the flames back to the fire itself. He remembers. He carries inside him a memory of the Australian Bushman, the Native American Indian, the cave dweller from a forgotten France. The memories vie with each other and merge in his body/mind. Suddenly, he gets up on his feet and he starts moving, swaying as if a spark from the fire had ignited his movement. The stars—billion-year-old spotlights—shine on him as he makes his first circle around the fire. A wolf, ten thousand years old, howls in the background as the would-be warrior responds to some primeval rhythm he hears playing inside his heart. Grabbing a long stick that looks like a spear, from the not-yet-burned wood he jabs it toward the flame and dances. Clock-time stands

185

still. Archetypal time paces the drama he is unknowingly enacting. He hears drums, he listens to stories being told by the old men, counsels with his fellow warriors, and then wakes up.

He gets up from a bed wet with sweat, washes his face, makes himself a cup of coffee, puts some wood in the woodstove, sits down, and weeps.

Six months later he finds himself in a men's group. A year later he attends his first men's gathering in the woods. He's hungry for something wild in him to emerge that he can befriend and use. He recalls that it was just this same hunger that drove him to drugs, alcohol, work, money, and sex. When he'd get stoned in the sixties, he'd take off all of his clothes and dance and yell and be timeless. Every time he did, though, he felt it to be artificial. He'd carry that feeling with him for days after each encounter with cannabis. It was just this need that led him to drink enough to be able to grab one of his buddies by the neck, and rub his head real hard while telling him how much "I love you, you son-of-a-bitch—you're the best friend in the world, give me another beer, will you." He'd chalk up any unusual display of emotion to "we were drunk."

There's a wildness in each man I've met that longs for the same kind of spontaneity and exuberance Thoreau searched for at Walden. There's a warrior in each man, a dancer in each accountant, construction worker, psychologist, and author who is readying to make an appearance around a fire, with drums in hand, grief in heart, and genuine, nonchemical ecstacy in his whole body. And it will be displayed at a wedding. A ceremony where the positive, healthy, patient father is united with a feminine, nurturing strong woman who waits within. With the best man by his side, the truly, deeply masculine merges with the deeply feminine, and the inner child is born.

Let the wedding, your father's and mine begin. Here comes the groom. Here comes the bride, all in one dancer, one warrior, one recovering, deeply masculine male.

# APPENDIXES

# APPENDIX I

## BOOKS

William Anderson and Clive Hicks, *Green Man*, Harper & Collins.
Robert Bly, *Iron John*, Addison Wesley.
Jean Shimoden Bolen, *Gods in Everyman*, Harper & Row.
Arthur Coleman and Libby Coleman, *The Father*, Chiron Publications
Guy Corneau, *Absent Father, Lost Sons*, Shambala.
Jed Diamond, *Inside Out*, Fifth Wave Press.
Warren Farrell, *The Liberated Man*, Bantam.
Herb Goldberg, *The Inner Male*, Signet.
Robert Hopche, *Men's Dreams, Men's Healings*, Shambala.
Robert Johnson, *He*, St. Martin's Press.
Sam Keen, *Fire in the Belly*, Bantam.
Etheridge Knight, *Born of a Woman*, Houghton Mifflin Co.
John Lee, *The Flying Boy*, Health Communications, Inc.
John Lee, *The Flying Boy II: The Journey Continues*, Health
   Communications, Inc.
John Lee, *Recovery: Plain and Simple*, Health Communications, Inc.
George Lough and John Sanford, *What Men Are Like*, Paulist Press.
Mickey Hart, *Drumming at the Edge of Magic*, Harper & Collins.
Robert Moore and Douglas Gillette, *King, Warrior, Magician, Lover*,
   Harper & Row.
Samuel Osherson, *Finding Our Fathers, Finding Ourselves*, The Free
   Press.
Joseph Pleck, *The Myth of Masculinity*, Prentice Hall.

# APPENDIX II

═══════════

## MAGAZINES

JOHN LEE is co-founder and publisher of *MAN!*, a quarterly magazine devoted to men's issues, relationships, and recovery. Subscriptions are $12.00/year, $3.50 newsstand, $4.50 back issues. Write to *MAN!* 1611 West 6th Street, Austin, TX 78703.

Other men's publications include:

*Changing Men: Issues in
Gender, Sex and Politics*,
$16.00/year
306 North Brooks
Madison, WI 53715

*Full-Time Dads*, $18.00 with
membership
P.O. Box 12773
St. Paul, MN 55112

*Icarus Revue*, $8.00/2 issues
P.O. Box 50174
Austin, TX 78763

*Inroads*, $7.50/2 issues
P.O. Box 14944
University Station
Minneapolis, MN 55414

*Journeymen*, $24.00/year
513 Chreater Turnpike
Candia, NH 03034

*Man Alive, A Journal of Men's Wellness*, $8.00/year (4 issues)
P.O. Box 40300
Albuquerque, NM 87196

*Men's Council Newsletter*,
$10.00/4 issues
P.O. Box 4795
Boulder, CO 80306

*Men Talk*, $14.00/year
Twin Cities Men's Center
3255 Hennepin Avenue South, Suite 45
Minneapolis, MN 55408

*The Men's Studies Review*,
$10.00/year
P.O. Box 32
Harriman, TN 37748

*Transitions*, free with $30.00 membership
National Coalition of Free Men
P.O. Box 129
Manhasset, NY 11030

*Wingspan*, free with donation (4 issues)
c/o Advantage Group
P.O. Box 1491
Manchester, MA 01944

# APPENDIX III

## AUDIOCASSETTES

**John Lee's Tapes**

*Why Men Can't Feel and the Price Women Pay*
*Expressing Your Anger Appropriately*
*Grieving, a Key to Healing*
*Healing the Father-Son Wound*
*What Co-Dependency Really Is*
*Addictive Relationships*
*Saying Good-bye to Mom and Dad*
*Couples, Caring, and Co-Dependency*
*The Flying Boy: Healing the Wounded Man Series*

**Other Recommended Tapes**

*An Evening with Robert Bly*
*Ancient Voices*, Joseph Campbell
*Beyond Dogma One*, Joseph Campbell
*Beyond Dogma Two*, Joseph Campbell
*DRUM! How to Play the Rhythms of Africa and Latin America*, Geoff Johns
*Fairy Tales for Men and Women*, Robert Bly
*Fathering the Boy Within*, James Snichowski
*HE: Understanding Masculine Psychology*, Robert A. Johnson

*Healing the Masculine*, Robert Moore
*Into the Deep: Male Mysteries*, Robert Bly
*Iron John and the Male Mode of Feeling*, Robert Bly
*Male Naivete and Giving the Gold Away with Robert Bly*
*Man of a Thousand Myths*, Joseph Campbell
*Men and the Life of Desire*, Robert Bly, James Hillman, and Michael
    Meade
*Men and the Wild Child*, Robert Bly and James Hillman
*Men and the Wound*, Robert Bly
*Myth as Metaphor*, Joseph Campbell
*Myth of the Fool*, Joseph Campbell
*Myth of the Fool II*, Joseph Campbell
*Off with the Rat's Head*, Michael Meade
*So My Soul Can Sing*, Etheridge Knight
*The Boy Who Married an Eagle*, Clarissa Pinkola Estes, Ph.D.
*The Healing Drum*, Yaya Diallo
*The Human Shadow*, Robert Bly
*The Lizard in the Fire*, Michael Meade
*The Power of Shame*, Robert Bly
*Warming the Stone Child*, Clarissa Pinkola Estes, Ph.D.

# APPENDIX IV

## MEN'S CENTERS

ARLINGTON MEN'S
COUNCIL
3102 Viscount Court
Annandale, VA 22003
Flemming Belrand
(703) 698–8496 (newsletter)

AUSTIN MEN'S CENTER
1611 West 6th Street
Austin, TX 78703
(512) 477–9595

AXIS COUNCIL
P.O. Box 1995
Ann Arbor, MI 48106

BALTIMORE MEN'S
COUNCIL
612 Overbrook Road
Bact, MD 21212
Tom Casciero
(301) 377–0041

COALITION OF 3 MEN
P.O. Box 129
Manhassett, NY 11030

COLORADO MEN'S
COUNCIL
P.O. Box 4795
Boulder, CO 80306

CORPUS CHRISTI MEN'S
CENTER
P.O. Box 331296
Corpus Christi, TX 78463
Marshall Hardy
(512) 887–8290

DALLAS MEN'S CENTER
811 L.B.J. Freeway, Suite 665
Dallas, TX 75251
Richard Carter, Ph.D.
(214) 234–6136 or
(214) 644–3691

FAIRFAX MEN'S COUNCIL
1809 Baldwin Drive
McLean, VA 22101
Furman Riley
(703) 968–7995

FREDRICKS MEN'S
COUNCIL
8002-B Dolly Hide Road
Mt. Airy, MD 21771
Bruce Barth
(301) 831–7060

GAITHERSBURG MEN'S
COUNCIL
12409 Keenland Place
Gaithersburg, MD 20878
Tom Golden
(301) 948–4692

LOS ANGELES MEN'S
CENTER
9012 Burton Way
Beverly Hills, CA 90212
Stephen Johnson, Ph.D.
(213) 276–9598

(MARYLAND) TALKING
STICK (*MAG QUARTERLY*)
182 Thomas Johnson Drive, #200
Fredrick, MD 21701

MEN'S CENTER FOR
COUNSELING AND
THERAPY
2925 Shattuck Avenue
Berkeley, CA 94705

MEN'S CENTER OF SAN
DIEGO
103 Highway 101, Suite 256
Encinitas, CA 92024
George Wolford
(619) 753–8463

MEN'S COUNCIL
Chapel Hill, NC
Fred Stevens
(919) 544–5764

MEN'S COUNCIL OF THE
HOUSTON AREA
5301 Memorial (at Aloe)
P.O. Box 980818
Houston, TX 77098
David Spaw
(713) 524–4149

MEN'S COUNCIL OF
WASHINGTON
2114 Belvedere Boulevard, #6
Silver Springs, MD 20902
Doug Giauque
(301) 593–8182
(largest in area, meetings with
200–300 men)

MEN'S RESOURCE HOTLINE
NATIONAL
P.O Box 882
San Anselmo, CA 94960
(415) 453–2839

MEN'S STUDIES COUNCIL /
ASSOCIATION
P.O. Box 32
Harriman, TN 37748
Jim Doyle

MEN'S WORK CENTER
1950 Sawtelle Boulevard
Suite 34
Los Angeles, CA 90025
James Snichowski
(213) 479–2749

MIDSOUTH MEN'S COUNCIL
6001 Knight Arnold Road
Memphis, TN 38115
Bill Hedzel
(901) 795–7387

3200 Medora Cove
Memphis TN 38118
Ralph Chumbley
(901) 362–3941

MINNESOTA MEN'S
COUNCIL
3255 Hennepin Avenue South
Suite 45
Minneapolis, MN 55408
(612) 822–5892

NATIONAL CONGRESS
OF MEN
2020 Pennsylvania Avenue
Washington, DC 20003

NATIONAL MEN'S
RESOURCE CENTER
P.O. Box 882
San Anselmo, CA 94960
(415) 488–9883

NATIONAL ORGANIZATION
FOR MEN AGAINST SEXISM
(NOMAS)
794 Pennsylvania Avenue
Pittsburgh, PA 15221

NETWORK
1241 East Chestnut, Suite D
Santa Ana, CA 92701

NEW YORK MEN'S COUNCIL
137 Clinton Avenue
Brooklyn, NY 11205
(718) 852–1567

NORTHERN SHENNANDOAH
VALLEY MEN'S COUNCIL
707 South Washington Street
Winchester, VA 22601
Jack Bellingham
(703) 667–6954

OAKLAND MEN'S PROJECT
440 Grand Avenue, Suite 320
Oakland, CA 94610
Charles Jones
(415) 835–2433

OMAHA PLATTE VALLEY
MEN'S COUNCIL
Omaha, NE
Steve Abraham
(402) 553–5976

PHOENIX CENTER FOR MEN
3620 Long Beach Boulevard
Suite C-1
Long Beach, CA 90807

RICHMOND AREA MEN'S
COUNCIL
P.O. Box 35613
Richmond, VA 23235
Dick Leatherman
(804) 320–2415

RICHMOND MEN'S
COUNCIL
Richmond, VA
(804) 282–6538

ROCKY MOUNTAIN MEN'S
CENTER
P.O. Box 6274
Boulder, CO 80306
Tom Daily
(303) 444–7797

SEATTLE MEN'S EVOLVING
NETWORK
602 West Howe Street
Seattle, WA 98119
Robert Carlson
(206) 285–4356 or
(206) 454–1787

TEXAS MEN'S CENTER
8012 Shinoak Drive
San Antonio, TX 78233
(512) 945–9112

TIDE WATER MEN'S
COUNCIL
1465 Lake James Drive
Virginia Beach, VA 23464
Bill Wright
(804) 523–9303

TULSA BROTHERHOOD
LODGES
701 South Cincinate
Tulsa, OK 74103

TWIN CITIES MEN'S CENTER
3255 Hennepin Avenue South
Suite 45
Minneapolis, MN 55408
*Men Talk* and *Inroads*
(magazines)
(612) 822–5892

WEST MICHIGAN MEN'S
ENRICHMENT CENTER
357 Covell Road Northwest
Grand Rapids, MI 49504
William B. Beidler
(800) 755–7720 or
(616) 453–7725

If you're interested in opening or
restructuring a men's center,
contact:

TEXAS PLANNING AND
REORGANIZATION
NETWORK
1611 West 6th Street
Austin, TX 78703

P.O. Box 5985
Austin, TX 78763
(512) 476-1611

## ABOUT THE AUTHOR

John Lee leads men's conferences and gatherings across the country, as well as seminars on codependence and adult children. The author of *The Flying Boy* and two other books, he is considered one of the leaders of the growing men's movement. He lives in Austin, Texas.